*PR*

# Divorce, holistically Yours

"Anyone contemplating divorce would do well to read and digest this comprehensive, practical, and inspiring guidebook that helps individuals and couples make decisions that reflect their deepest values and integrity and that honor the holistic needs of each family member.

After clearly describing the steps of the divorce process, Pamela takes readers on an empowering journey of self-awareness that can turn a once-frightening event into a catalyst for greater life, love, joy, healing, and peace. Pamela's keen legal mind and calm, compassionate presence provide readers with clarity, comfort, and confidence to help them minimize the pitfalls and maximize the potentials in divorce.

This rare integration of legal realities with enlightened, holistic approaches to wellbeing belongs in the hands of all those who are considering, are experiencing, or have experienced divorce, as well as the professionals who serve them. Divorce really can be a portal to greater awakening and fulfillment. This is a grounded, transformational guidebook that no divorcing person should be without."

*– Rebecca Wells Windinwood, M.A., L.M.F.T., S.E.P.*

"Thank you, Pamela, for *Divorce, Holistically Yours*. It is a book which had to be written, and which absolutely must be read — read not just by those who are divorcing, but also by everyone seeking to better understand their relationships and are in search of personal healing, development, and direction.

Pamela shares priceless, practical legal information which de-mystifies the legal process — integrated with, and balanced by, the holistic perspectives, possibilities and motivations for individual healing and growth.

I can say without reservation that this book gives readers a broad scope of practical legal knowledge and insightful wisdom well beyond what could be conveyed to clients during an initial consultation costing many times the price of this book."

— *C.M. Jorgenson, Esq., Family Law Litigator*

"A thoroughly informative, supportive and necessary text for anyone going through divorce. Readers are given invaluable legal knowledge that is critical to a successful divorce experience. Pamela fully describes the legal process and divorce options available in an easy-to-understand manner and describes how this event can be an opportunity to grow and heal from trauma. Use the concepts and tools presented to arm yourself with the knowledge you need to choose the best path, protect yourself and your family, and avoid an ugly divorce.

Divorce has only been known to me through years as a family lawyer. I received an unexpected benefit while reading this life-changing book. I was at a time of crisis in my own life and by using the advice, exercises and spiritual concepts, I was safely ushered back to the light. Pamela's extensive training and education have not only brought forth a guidebook that divorcing individuals and couples can use to survive their divorce — its healing value is pertinent to anyone."

— *Cherise Cuevas Loy, Esq., Family Lawyer*

"*Divorce, Holistically Yours* is a must read for those challenged with divorce. In clear, concise prose, Pamela demystifies the jargon, procedures, and options available — how some divorce processes can expose vulnerabilities and do further harm, while others can support emotional, spiritual, and mental healing. Pamela encourages those who are open to exploring different avenues of spiritual growth, to discover how their divorce may actually help them to move forward with grace, equanimity and hope."

*— Lynn R. Fletcher, Esq. Family Law Lawyer and Mediator*

"Pamela brought a career's worth of legal know-how with a refreshing dose of self-reflection and humanity to get me through the many legal, financial, and emotional challenges of my divorce. I am thrilled that Pamela's legal knowledge, insight and stabilizing guidance is now available to anyone going through the pain and uncertainty of dissolving a marriage."

*— Christine, Former Client*

"An essential guide to both the legal process and human process that will impact you deep within your soul. Pamela was instrumental in helping me separate the past from the path forward in a way that was both healing and liberating. If you are considering a divorce … or continue to struggle with the aftermath of a divorce, the information in this book, if read with an open mind, will indeed broaden your perspective. Divorce was one of the most difficult experiences in my life, but Pamela helped me navigate the process and come out the other side stronger, at peace, and eager to co-create my future vision."

*— Michael, Former Client, Father, Former husband, and CEO*

# Divorce, Holistically Yours

## Learn Essential Knowledge of the Legal Process

### and

## How Divorce Can Be a Catalyst for Your Soul's Evolution

### Pamela M. Pacetti

*Intuitive Attorney – Mediator – Coach*

Bridges to Spirit
P.O. Box 631
Redondo Beach CA 90277
Info@BridgestoSpirit.com

First Edition

Editing by Linda Jay
Book design by Val Sherer
Cover design by Deborah Perdue

Library of Congress Control Number: 2021910965

ISBN (Print) 978-0-578-89375-4
ISBN (e-Book) 978-0-578-89376-1

PRINTED IN THE UNITED STATES OF AMERICA

This project is dedicated to you, Dad. Although our time together was brief, your love endures. Thank you for continuing to shine your light and for celebrating the joyous times and moments of accomplishment, as well as guiding me through the obstacles of life. As the jewels of wisdom collected along my journey are shared with others, I send gratitude and love to you for your contributions.

Sending much love and gratitude to you, Mom, for your love and continued support and guidance. Although I miss you here, I am delighted to know the two of you are reunited in love.

# Contents

# PART I [B]
# The Four Processes of Divorce ........... 59

# PART II
# The Soul's Journey ....................... 107

# Foreword

Every journey in life is more meaningful in the hands of a profoundly wise and experienced guide, and the journey of divorce can be one of life's most challenging events. Having worked as a domestic relations attorney for over forty years, I have handled many complex divorce matters in Colorado, Virginia, and the District of Columbia. I have worked with hundreds of family law attorneys and professionals. Although I have received numerous awards, held several positions in local, state, and national organizations, drafted legislation, and have been recognized as "best family law attorney" in multiple publications year after year, I can say without reservation that working with Pamela has been one of the true highlights of my career.

I have had the privilege of working with Pamela in a professional capacity for over twenty years — both as an opposing counsel in divorce matters, and for several years as a fellow board member of the statewide organization for collaborative professionals. Pamela is highly respected in the community and has been a strong and constant advocate for change of how families are treated in divorce. She guides individuals to resolutions that others would deem impossible. Her enlightened, holistic perspective, coupled with her mastery of negotiation, the law and spirituality, make her uniquely qualified to provide guidance through the divorce process.

In *Divorce, Holistically Yours,* Pamela provides the reader with an intimate, yet comprehensive, guidebook of the legal process, and then expands this teaching with an innovative, holistic approach to the care and healing of the self during and after the divorce.

Part I is a concise and thought-provoking insider's guide to what really goes on behind the scenes in a divorce. Detailed information concerning property distribution, child and spousal support, custody matters, the litigation process, alternative approaches available, how to select the right attorney, and everything else the reader should know, is laid out in a way that only a seasoned professional can offer. Pamela has condensed many years of practice and wisdom into this guidebook that will inform and empower the reader. This is essential reading for anyone going through or contemplating divorce.

In Part II, Pamela's masterful writing takes the reader on an exploration of how divorce can be a catalyst to one's evolutionary growth and can bring about deep healing. The reader is encouraged to keep an open heart and mind as this book unfolds; however, even those unfamiliar with the concepts shared in these pages will most certainly come away with an enlightened perspective of themselves, their relationships with others, and the journey of their soul.

Divorce is indeed a life changing event, and *Divorce, Holistically Yours,* will forever change how you view yourself, your very existence, and how the unseen world plays a critical role in our evolutionary process.

— *Albert M. Bonin, Esquire*

# Introduction

Thank you for inviting me on your divorce journey. Whether you are the one initiating a divorce, or it is your spouse who has turned the wheel in that direction, I am honored that you have chosen this book as a tool to assist your movement forward. Although I cannot personally be with you on your journey, know that I have written this book to read as though I am present with you, guiding you, and sharing with you all of the information and experience I can to assist you each step of the way. We all understand that information is power. When we are faced with the transition of divorce, the more we know, the more we can remain balanced and can begin making long-term decisions from a place of clarity rather than from a place of confusion.

This book is divided into two parts. In Part I, we will cover the elements of the divorce process you must know before you embark on your divorce journey. We will cover the role of the court system in the divorce process and how the laws dealing with divorce are established and how they might affect your case. We will cover the primary issues that require resolution in the divorce process, including property distribution, financial support issues, and issues related to child custody.

We will cover how to best choose an attorney to represent your interests in the divorce and what you need to gather in preparation for the journey. We will take an honest, in-depth look at the litigation process, and will then cover three alternative approaches to the traditional litigation process for you to consider. I have shared as much as I can in these pages of what I have learned from over twenty years of representing clients through their journeys of divorce. Please understand that some of the information that is shared in Part I may be dry, and may challenge your attention span; however, remember that this information is not meant to entertain you, but rather to educate and empower you. You will reach in Part I a level of knowledge and understanding that will prevent many hours of needless confusion. Moreover, this book will help you become a true partner with your attorney, thereby making communication and planning more productive.

In Part II, we will dive into the soul's journey and discover how the divorce process can actually be a catalyst for your soul's evolution. Whether you have been on a spiritual journey for some time or whether the divorce process, together with the offerings in this book, serves to jump-start your spiritual journey, you will come away from the experience with an expanded awareness. You will view yourself, as well as your divorce, from an entirely new perspective. Those who have a good understanding of the role of the court system, and a foundation in the law of their jurisdiction, have hand-picked the right attorney to work with, have chosen a divorce process that is best suited for their personality and the factors in their case, and, most importantly, are willing to engage in the inner work recommended in this book, will have a very different divorce experience than the majority who have traveled this road before them.

Those who are willing to use the information provided in these pages and engage with the right intention and with an open heart, will look back on their divorce as one of the most enlightening and profound experiences they have engaged in, as it relates to their personal and spiritual growth. The collateral blessings that come from the experience will be equally profound. Whether in the form of the reader's overall well-being, the well-being of the children involved in the divorce, or the effects on extended family members, friends, colleagues, and future relationships, the blessings that come from an enlightened perspective are vast and meaningful.

Although a book concentrating on divorce can never cover every contingency and fact pattern that you may experience during your divorce, the information in these pages was chosen to provide you with what you need to take control over your divorce, rather than allowing the divorce process to control you. Moreover, it will allow you to experience your divorce from the roadmap of your soul, which is waiting to lovingly lead you to a new beginning. When divorce is innately viewed as a beginning rather than as an ending, the journey becomes one of grace and anticipation, imbued with self-confidence. All transitions come with uncertainty; however, when we are willing to explore beyond the illusion and focus our attention on the true agenda of the soul, we are met with an abundance of assistance and therefore reach a place of clarity much sooner.

It is with humility that I ask you to read the words in this book with an open heart and mind. If you read something that does not resonate with you after some reflection, then simply let it go and move on to the next offering. An enlightened perspective is one which is open and not afraid to either accept or reject information that is brought to one's awareness. There are many things we hear and immediately reject, based upon our individual beliefs, life experiences and patterns; however, when we appreciate that certain information finds its way to us at the time we need it most, we are more inclined to contemplate and work with the information, as opposed to immediately disregarding it as not important or suited for us.

If you have been searching for a tool to assist you in your divorce, and this book was presented to you, there is most certainly something within these pages that is meant for you. As someone who has been a practicing divorce attorney for many years, I have a seasoned understanding of both the divorce process and the impact it has on the individuals going through it. As someone who has been on a spiritual journey most of my adult life, I have an intimate understanding of how the events in our life, divorce being a major one, are put in our path for a specific reason. The higher purpose of these transitional events is typically a mystery to our human understanding — that is, unless we are willing to do the work to uncover the reasons and the blessings. Once we are empowered by these revelations, we become inspired and naturally have a new desire to move forward on our journey.

It is my intention and desire that the information in this book will provide you with the support you need to gently navigate your way through the process of divorce. As we embark on this journey together, let's set the intention together that you are safe, that the information and tools in this book will help you reach the other side of your divorce feeling comfortably content with the outcome — inspired, healed (or well on your way to healing), enlightened, grateful, ready to embark on the next phase of your journey, and most importantly, appreciating a deeper understanding of who you really are.

### *And So It Is!*

# PART I - [A]

# The Legal Process of Divorce

# 1

# The Legal Side of Divorce

Whether you are contemplating divorce, or you suspect your spouse is, there is important information that you need to know at the outset. In addition to dissolving the bonds of matrimony, the divorce process includes: the division of marital property, which is commonly referred to as the marital estate; resolving legal and physical custody of any minor children of the marriage; and, in certain cases, the determination of whether financial support will be payable by one spouse to the other. It is important to understand the law in your particular jurisdiction; this is best accomplished by a thorough consultation with an attorney in your area. I will be discussing how to best choose an attorney in Chapter 6. For most individuals, the divorce process is an unknown that elicits fear and triggers one's deepest insecurities. To obviate the fear and to shift the mystery of divorce into a tangible and workable roadmap, it is vital to prepare yourself for the journey. This is done by seeking knowledge from reputable professionals and avoiding making assumptions about your divorce based upon what you have previously observed, experienced, or heard from others about their divorce experience.

## *The Greek Chorus*

The instinct to talk to friends, family members, and colleagues, is natural when we are going through an important life transition. However, it is important to keep the information gained from these discussions in perspective. Advice, support, and the sharing of stories from family, friends and perhaps colleagues, is referred to as, "the Greek Chorus." The input from others can be equally as harmful to your journey as helpful. There are certainly times when we feel the need to reach out to others if we are facing a challenging event in our life. However, we must be careful to not allow words from others, even when said with well-meaning intentions, to cloud our judgment and prevent us from making decisions that truly reflect who we are at our core. Ultimately, we are responsible for making our own choices, and we must live with the consequences of those decisions. It is fine to share and to seek advice from others we trust; however, it is important to keep the information we receive from these exchanges in perspective. When we allow too much input from outside sources, we ignore our inner dialogue and run the risk of making decisions based on *what we think is expected of us, rather than what is actually in our own highest good.*

Should you choose to have conversations concerning your divorce, please reject the impulse to do so when you are feeling anxious, sad, fearful, or any other emotion that will color your perception. Always "feel" into what is being shared with you and ask yourself whether the information truly resonates with you. Does it elevate your energy, or does it trigger fear and other lower-energy vibrations? If you feel inspired, and come away from the discussion feeling balanced and empowered, then use the information gained as talking points to share with your legal counsel.

Many individuals would like a second chance to redo their own divorce and will attempt to work vicariously through you as a tool. Divorce is certainly a time when many lose their balance, their trust and belief in themselves, their confidence, and their ability to visualize a path forward. It is through awareness, and the ability to step out of the space of uncertainty, that the path will begin to reveal itself. The first step is to gain pertinent knowledge of the process, and to understand that your divorce is unique to you and your family — this perspective must be maintained throughout the process. It cannot be stressed enough, that what is right for one individual or family may *not* be right for another.

## *The Development of Laws Related to Divorce*

Divorce is a legal process; therefore, there must be laws and procedures in place to accommodate the citizens who require the operation of the law. Reduced to the most common denominator, divorce is simply the dissolution of the matrimonial bonds between two individuals. Historically, courts in this country could only grant a divorce based upon traditional grounds of serious breaches of the marriage contract — such as adultery, desertion, and cruelty. By statute in most states, absent clear proof of these grounds, mere incompatibility of the parties or simple dissatisfaction with the marriage were insufficient reasons for courts to dissolve the marriage. In 1969, the California legislature was the first to pass "no-fault divorce" laws, permitting parties to divorce without alleging and proving traditional grounds. Every state now has "no-fault" divorce procedures, and eighteen U.S. states are now granting divorces exclusively on a "no-fault" basis.

However, current laws permitting this less-hostile process require expiration of a "waiting period" after the date of the parties' final separation before a court can issue a final divorce decree. States have different waiting periods; some are longer if the parties have minor children. Where still permitted, grounds-based divorces are still sought today. Whether a party seeks a divorce based on grounds, where permitted, or a no-fault divorce based simply upon incompatibility and irreconcilable differences, will depend on the facts and circumstances of each case.

The issues that are handled simultaneously — property division, custody, and support matters — are subset issues of the divorce itself. Accordingly, there are laws that are pertinent to the dissolution of the marriage itself, and there are laws dealing with the subset issues, for those unable to reach a resolution without the court's intervention.

To step in and assist in these areas, the court must have a framework from which to make these determinations. This is a much broader discussion than what can be shared here; however, it is important to provide a taste of how the legal process works, so that you can begin to build your own framework from which to proceed. When we are aware that we have options and can take control over these very personal issues, we are less inclined to entirely surrender to this seemingly "fated" process.

Briefly explained, the legislature of each state codifies the framework for each of these issues. As cases are tried in a court setting, the judge applies this framework to the facts of each case in order to make a determination. Over time, these cases do provide direction for how other cases with similar fact patterns should be interpreted and ruled upon. Pausing here for a moment, one can begin to see how unique facts of each case provide the ingredients from which the judge seeks to match or blend with the basic framework in order to craft a determination.

Certain patterns begin to develop, so that even the slightest similarity might be stretched enough to yield the same results, but it is important to understand that the patterns referred to are distinct issues and not overall family patterns. A quick example might include a family decision made during the marriage for one spouse to give up, or set aside, a career in order to serve as the main caretaker of the children. There are a plethora of reasons that might have precipitated this family decision. At the time of the divorce, this issue may seem quite common; however, the facts and circumstances will be very different for each family. It stands to reason that the pendulum of resolution can swing quite widely in how the court might treat this issue. Similarly, the differences in a fact pattern may be so disparate from established determinations that the seemingly applicable case law will not apply. In these cases, the sitting judge will be tasked to interpret the law and the facts presented in order to reach what is commonly referred to as *a case of first impression.*

Clearly, no matter what the issues are, no two cases are alike. One family's facts and circumstances will naturally be different from another family's. Even when there are similarities and seasoned case law has addressed these issues, arguments may be proffered that may mean that an alternative application of the law should prevail.

There is no better play on the phrase, "It is all up for interpretation," than in the court system. Case law is fluid, constantly changing. Individuals who are unhappy with a court's interpretation of the law may appeal the decision. The appeals court may affirm a certain ruling by finding it to be consistent with case law and/or within the judge's discretion, or it may remand (send back) one or more issues to the trial court, with instructions, meaning another expensive bite of the apple. What this does for the legal industry is provide tighter guidelines from which to predict certain outcomes.

But, for the parties engaged personally in the process, this highlights the margin for error, and that one judge's interpretation of the law, and use of his or her discretion, may be completely different from another judge's — including judges sitting in the same courthouse. The number of judges presiding over these cases is determined by the size of the jurisdiction's population. This is not to say that the court system is broken or flawed; rather, it highlights the importance of divorcing parties understanding that the courtroom is rarely the optimal choice for determining what is best for a family in transition. Whether it be property division, child custody matters, or support matters, the court system does the best it can within the framework and case law available. However, considering the uniqueness of each family, any attempt to design a judicial one-size-fits-all approach is simply not feasible. In fact, some decisions concerning family law matters can appear to be somewhat draconian in nature, at least in terms of their results.

I have attempted to provide as much information as I can in these pages so that you feel confident in your own divorce matter. I understand that some of the information will seem very dry; that is to be expected. However, rest assured, that the more you understand the system, the better you will be at preparing yourself, your expectations, and your ability to make pertinent decisions concerning your case as it proceeds.

# 2

# The Marital Estate

The following chapters are intended to provide a general understanding of the main issues to be resolved in the divorce process. We will start with a discussion of how the marital estate is typically defined and treated. We will then discuss the information you should know, and the documents you should gather concerning this issue, preferably prior to having a consultation with an attorney. We will then discuss the issues of spousal support, child custody and child support.

Whether a jurisdiction uses the term, "equitable distribution," "community property," "common law," or an alternate name to describe the method used to divide the marital estate, the first step is to classify a certain property into "marital property," "separate property," or "part-marital and part-separate property," sometimes referred to as, "hybrid property." Once property has been properly classified, the case law in a particular jurisdiction is then used to determine how that property will be treated and divided between the spouses. Marital property usually includes all property earned and/or acquired by either party, from the date of marriage until the date of separation, or, in some instances, until the date of divorce. Separate property usually includes all property earned and/or acquired by one spouse *prior* to the date of marriage or *after* the date of separation, and typically includes inherited or gifted property that a spouse received *at any time*.

However, it is important to know that certain decisions that were made during the marriage might alter the classification of property. As an example, if the parties used the inherited funds of one spouse for the down payment on their marital residence, and thereafter made monthly mortgage payments from the income earned by either party, the residence might be classified as a hybrid property at the time of the divorce. The separate nature of the inherited property was commingled with marital funds, thus altering its original classification. How the separate contribution will be treated depends on several factors, and is unique to each jurisdiction. In some cases, if the separate property can be traced back to a source that would be classified as separate property — in our example, the inherited property — it may be credited to the spouse who inherited it by any number of formulas used by a particular jurisdiction.

Sometimes the actions of the parties during the marriage serve to completely transmute property from one classification to another. In our example, the parties may have refinanced the property several times, or even sold and repurchased another property with the proceeds. The more complicated the fact pattern, the more complicated the issue becomes. In this example, the party who contributed the inherited funds will want credit for his or her separate contributions, while the other party will push to change the classification of the inherited property into marital property.

It is important to make no assumptions concerning how property will be classified and ultimately distributed by a court. This includes assumptions based upon how property is titled, be it individually or jointly. Whether marital property will be equally or unequally divided, whether separate property will remain separate, whether hybrid property will be treated as hybrid in the distribution or will be considered transmuted from marital to separate or from separate to marital — each decision is unique to the fact pattern of each case. This discussion is to serve not only as a rough guideline as to how certain property may be classified and treated, but also to illustrate the complexity involved in the distribution of the marital estate. The facts and circumstances unique to your case will be fleshed out further by the attorney you choose to engage within your jurisdiction. The more information and documentation you have, the better your attorney will be able to discuss potential outcomes during your consultation.

It is extremely important that you understand the financial picture of your marriage. There are many families in which one spouse surrenders the financial affairs and decisions to the other during the marriage. Even if both of you are engaged in the financial operation of the marriage, it is imperative that you begin to gather as much information as possible prior to the commencement of a divorce action. In this instance, knowledge is not only power, but also necessary in order to have equilibrium between the parties in terms of the details.

A major cause of the fear that attaches to the divorce process is partly due to a lack of knowledge. The more information you can gather at the outset, the better. The following is a typical list of the information that you should gather, copy, and bring with you to your consultation with an attorney. This documentation applies to assets owned by both spouses. Whether an account statement or another document is titled jointly or in the individual name of only one spouse, it is all relevant; leave nothing out.

- Checking and Savings Account Statements
- Mutual Funds
- Stocks and Bonds
- Pension Statements
- 401(K) Statements
- Individual Retirement Account Statements
- Deeds of Trust (mortgage statements) on all real property
- Financial Statements that have been completed by one or both parties (e.g., for a home loan, car loan, business loan, or any other lending institution)
- Credit Card Statements
- Promissory Notes and other Debt Instruments
- Documents / Closing Statements related to the acquisition of the marital residence and any investment or vacation properties
- Documents / Closing Statements for the sale of any real property during the marriage
- Individual and Joint Income Tax Returns for the past three-to-five years
- Income Information, such as paystubs, 1099s, W-2s, K-1s, rental income, interest income, family gifts, lottery winnings, etc. (Income is defined very broadly in most jurisdictions — if you have any doubt, include it)
- Health Insurance Policies and Premiums

- Life Insurance Policies

- Documents related to Automobiles, Recreational Vehicles, Planes, Boats, and other similar assets

- Documents related to Investment Property, such as Art, Rugs, Jewelry, Antiques, Collections, and other similar assets

- Family Business Documentation: Tax Returns for the past three-to-five years, balance sheets, profit-and-loss statements, buy-sell agreements, leases, closing statements for any real property owned by the business, inventory list(s), etc.

Do not worry if you are unable to gather all the information listed above prior to your consultation with your attorney. It is important to gather what you can in the initial stages so that you are not spending most of your time and money in the formal discovery process discussed in Chapter 7. Your attorney will be in a better position to make recommendations and move the case forward if he or she understands the marital assets and liabilities in the early stages of the case.

# 3

# Spousal Support / Maintenance

The dissolution of a marriage does not automatically terminate the financial obligations of the parties to each other. Spousal support or spousal maintenance, sometimes referred to as alimony, is an award of financial support payable by one spouse to the other. The main purpose of a spousal support award is to provide the spouse who is earning no income, or much less than the higher earning spouse, the financial resources necessary to maintain a standard of living similar to that enjoyed by the parties during the marriage. There are as many circumstances that may cause a need for spousal support as there are marriages. A spouse may have set aside his or her education and/or career to support the career aspirations of the other spouse. One spouse may have lost his or her ability to earn a living due to an unforeseen illness. Perhaps one party stepped away from his or her employment, either partly or completely, to care for the children of the marriage. A spouse who is denied financial support in any of these circumstances might face financial hardship following a divorce.

For the parties, the issue of spousal support can trigger deep seated fear. Whether a party is the higher-earning spouse, who is fearful that he or she may lose a portion of their future income, or the lesser-earning spouse, who will be dependent on the financial support of the other party, the fear associated with the implications of this reality can be quite raw. To put this issue in perspective, most courts consider the marriage akin to a business partnership. Each party performed their roles during the partnership, be it well or poorly. However, when the business relationship is severed, absent an agreement, both parties are entitled to a fair share of the wealth accumulated – or, as in the case of spousal support, the earning ability of the parties.

In a marriage, it is quite common for one party to contribute more of the monetary support for the family, while the other party performs more of the non-monetary support. In the eyes of most jurisdictions, absent extreme circumstances, these distinct contributions are weighed equally, and both are considered necessary for the marriage partnership to thrive. When discussions ensue concerning a monetary value that might be placed on the non-monetary contributions, it is easier to appreciate and understand why these non-monetary contributions have value. If the spouse who performed these contributions during the marriage received a salary for his or her services, the marital estate might have increased in value. Similarly, if the partnership would have paid for each of these services, the marital estate might be further depleted. Moreover, if, rather than performing these non-monetary contributions, that spouse was employed during the marriage, both spouses would have a much greater income potential at the time of the divorce, and their needs for support might be lessened. The spouse who sacrificed his or her career and instead devoted his or her energy to the non-monetary contributions to the marriage partnership, will most likely be dependent upon their spouse for financial support following a divorce. Thus, the "fairness" of a court in understanding the equality in the monetary and non-monetary contributions of the parties becomes clearer.

Most jurisdictions have statutes that include enumerated factors a court must consider when making a spousal support determination. A spousal support award is not mandatory, but rather, a discretionary decision made upon an analysis of the factors of each case. Examples include the age and physical and mental health of the parties, education, training, earning potentials, the length of marriage, financial decisions made during the marriage, the standard of living during the marriage, tax implications, the income potential from real property or other assets that will be financially owned by each of the parties following the divorce, the financial obligations of each of the parties, and any other factors a court might consider relevant in making a determination.

A spouse requesting support is expected, in most jurisdictions, to earn as much income as he or she is capable of earning. Thus, if a spouse chose to work part-time during the marriage, but is capable of working full-time, and a full-time position is available, a court may impute or artificially raise the income of that party to the salary that would be attributable to a full-time position when making a final support determination. In some jurisdictions, a court may not impute income to a non-working parent with primary physical custody of a child below school age. The concept of highest earning potential also applies to the higher-earning spouse. That spouse would not be permitted to modify his or her schedule from full-time to part-time, or to change employment if such underemployment or new employment could prevent them from providing needed support to their spouse. In this instance, the court could impute or artificially raise the amount of income the party earned at his or her previous full-time status or previous employment. This concept is applicable to those who are self-employed; however, there is more analysis necessary to determine the true income of a self-employed spouse as opposed to the salary, bonuses and other potential perks one might receive from a traditional employment package.

## *Four Types of Spousal Support*
### *Temporary Support*

There are four types of spousal support. The first is known as temporary, preliminary, or *pendente lite* support. The divorcing parties are often living in separate residences during the divorce process. To maintain the status quo, a spouse may be ordered to pay spousal support to the lesser-earning spouse so that mortgages, rents, and other living expenses will be covered until the final hearing. Moreover, some jurisdictions may order the higher-earning spouse to provide funds so the lesser-earning spouse can pay attorney's fees and have the same access to representation. These initial awards, however, are not intended to cover a party's attorney's fees throughout the case. If the case proceeds to trial, there may be an additional monetary award intended to subsidize the attorney's fees paid by the lesser-earning spouse.

SPOUSAL SUPPORT / MAINTENANCE

## Rehabilitative Support

The second type of spousal support is known as rehabilitative support. Rehabilitative support is awarded mainly in shorter-term marriages and is intended to provide the lower income earner adequate time to become more self-sufficient. As an example, if a spouse stepped away from a nursing career for a period of time to provide care for the parties' children, that spouse may be awarded temporary support for the time needed to re-license, if applicable, and to find full-time employment.

## Permanent Support

The third type of spousal support is known as permanent spousal support. A permanent support award is typically reserved for longer-term marriages. However, a permanent award may be granted in a shorter marriage if one of the parties experienced an illness or an accident during the marriage that inhibits their ability to earn enough income to be self-sufficient. If the higher-earning spouse has the means to provide the necessary support, he or she may be ordered to do so, despite the length of the marriage. In most cases, in addition to a long-term marriage, there must be a large enough discrepancy in the income of the spouses to justify an award of support. The closer the income potential is for the parties, the less likely a court would order permanent support payable by one spouse to the other. For a permanent support order to be granted, the court must find that the analysis of the relevant factors in their jurisdiction, on balance, warrant an award of support for an indefinite duration. Without a

27

defined duration, the support obligation will continue until there is a terminating event, or an event that warrants a modification.

## Lump Sum Support

The final type of spousal support is referred to as a lump sum. A lump-sum award is a certain or fixed amount awarded to the receiving spouse. The court may order the paying spouse to make one lump-sum payment to satisfy the amount of the award, or the order may provide a series of payments to be made, each at a specified date. A lump-sum award has some advantages. For the paying spouse, he or she is not subject to the uncertainty attached to a monthly spousal support award, which has no pre-determined duration, as is typically awarded in longer-term marriages. With the lump-sum award, as soon as the amount is paid in full, the spousal support obligation of the paying spouse is automatically terminated. For the receiving spouse, he or she is not subject to the frequency and uncertainly of monthly payments, which may be subject to a future modification in the event of a material change of circumstances. Moreover, for those jurisdictions with statutes providing for the termination of a permanent spousal support obligation upon the remarriage of the receiving spouse, or the death of either party, a lump-sum award will likely survive these events.

Be sure to discuss both the advantages and disadvantages of each option with your attorney and tax advisor if the issue of spousal support will be negotiated outside of court.

## *Termination and Modification*

Court-ordered spousal support, other than a lump-sum award, carries uncertainty, in that the award remains modifiable and can be terminated as a matter of law in certain circumstances. A material change of circumstance by either party may trigger a modification, or in some cases, a complete termination. A jurisdiction's statute sets forth predetermined events that will automatically terminate a party's spousal support obligation. These events typically include the death of either party, the remarriage of the spouse receiving the support, or upon the receiving spouse's cohabitation with another individual for a period of time that, in the eyes of the law, is considered analogous to marriage. The death of a party can be easily ascertained in most cases. The receiving spouse has a duty to inform the paying spouse of his or her remarriage, thus relieving the paying spouse of the duty to monitor the life events of the receiving spouse. However, in those jurisdictions that provide for termination by cohabitation, the paying spouse must prove that the receiving spouse has been cohabitating with another individual for the specified period, and that such cohabitation meets the "analogous to marriage" requirement. This puts the expense and the burden of seeking evidence on the paying spouse, in those jurisdictions that do not also charge the receiving spouse with the duty to disclose their cohabitation.

Several events may trigger a party to request a modification of the spousal support award. The paying party may experience an involuntary reduction of income, or reach a certain age and wish to retire. The receiving party may experience an increase in earned income that might trigger a reduction in the amount of spousal support he or she receives from the other party. In addition, the receiving party might experience unforeseen expenses that were not present at the time of the initial award, and may wish to petition for an increase of support. It is important to note that, in most jurisdictions, the change of circumstances raised by a party requesting a modification of support must be deemed "material" by the court. As an example, an increase of ten percent in the earned income of the receiving spouse, or similarly, a reduction of ten percent in the earned income of the paying spouse, might not be considered material enough to warrant a modification to the existing support award.

# 4

# Child Custody

The standard used by most jurisdictions when determining child custody matters is known as, "the best interests of the child." This means that the focus of the court shall be to design a parenting arrangement that meets the best interests of the children, and not necessarily of the parents. There are two components to a custody determination — legal custody, and physical custody. Legal custody deals with who will have the right and responsibility to make decisions concerning the health, education, and overall well-being of the children. Physical custody concerns the day-to-day care of the children, and where they will primarily reside. When parties are unable to create a workable parenting plan outside of the court system, the court will evaluate several factors, and, using the best interests of the child standard, will create a parenting arrangement for them.

The following paragraphs are intended to provide an overview of what courts consider when determining a child custody matter, and how they might rule on the issue of legal and/or physical custody based upon the evidence presented.

## *Legal Custody*

With regard to legal custody, a court will typically award joint legal custody of the children. This means that both parties will continue to have a voice and decision-making authority when it comes to important legal decisions concerning their children. Courts expect the parents to consult and consent on these matters. On the other hand, the more contentious the parties are, the less likely they would exhibit the skills necessary to make joint legal decisions concerning their children. In this instance, the court may find it in the best interests of the children to assign decision-making authority to only one parent, thus providing one parent with sole legal custody or primary legal custody of the children. With sole legal custody, a parent can make any decision that falls under the umbrella of legal custody — as opposed to merely day-to-day decisions such as setting a bedtime when the children are in a party's care — without a discussion, input, or approval from the other parent.

Losing the right to make critical decisions concerning a child's education, medical needs, religious orientation, and the many other important decisions relating to raising children, might seem like a harsh result, but it is a very real consequence of a highly contentious divorce. It stands to reason that a judge charged with making decisions based upon the best interests of the children would not feel comfortable subjecting the children to a constant battle of wills when it comes to their well-being. It is more common to receive a joint legal custody determination; however, both parties must consider the power of the court to rule otherwise, and what it truly means to hand over these intimate decisions to a third party. The divorce process will eventually end, but the orders of the court regarding custody will live far beyond the time it takes for the animosity of the often-contentious process to subside.

## *Sole Physical Custody*

When determining physical custody, the court's focus remains on creating a parenting arrangement that will be in the best interests of the children. The court may award sole physical custody, sometimes referred to as sole primary physical custody, to one parent. This means that the children will primarily reside with one parent, subject to a court-imposed visitation/parenting schedule awarded to the non-custodial parent. It is important to note that, under these circumstances, the visitation schedule is typically a very standard schedule that might include every other weekend, one or two dinner visits during the week, an average of two weeks during the summer months (either consecutive or non-consecutive, depending on the age of the children and other considerations), and an alternating holiday schedule. The goal of the court is to foster some consistency for the children and to create a schedule that leaves little-to-no room for misinterpretation by the parents.

The court is certainly free to, and often does, insert additional terms into the visitation schedule, such as a nightly telephone call with the children when they are in the care of the other parent. The award of a scheduled nightly telephone call is often misinterpreted by most parents. That telephone call is for the benefit of the children. It is always important for children to feel a sense of connection to both of their parents since, following a divorce, children are seldom in the company of both parents at the same time. It is for this purpose that most courts will view this right as belonging to the children. A daily telephone call with an absent parent to review the day and/or participate in a goodnight ritual will provide a child with a sense of connection to that absent parent, and will lessen any feelings of abandonment or anxiety a child might be experiencing.

Another term may be to award each parent a first "right of refusal" to care for the children when the parent with scheduled parenting time is unable to do so. This right will be triggered if a parent is unable to care for the children for a certain number of hours, as pre-determined by the court. In some cases, this right may be reserved for those times in which a parent is unable to care for the children for an overnight period.

It cannot be stressed enough that a court-ordered parenting arrangement is rarely conducive to the operation of most families. A common example includes the children's participation in extracurricular activities. If a certain activity chosen by one parent interferes with the other parent's scheduled parenting time, the children will be unable to engage in that activity, without consent from that parent. It seems counterintuitive that a parent might withhold his or her agreement for a child to engage in a desired extracurricular activity; however, a party with limited parenting time might prefer an alternative way of allocating quality time.

## Shared Physical Custody

The court may also award shared physical custody, sometimes referred to as joint primary custody. In this instance, the children will reside with both parents, in accordance with a court-imposed schedule. There are several possible shared schedules. Depending on the age of the children, the court may order an alternating weekly schedule, whereby the children are in the primary care of one parent from Sunday evening to the next Sunday evening; they will then be in the care of the other parent from that Sunday evening to the following Sunday evening, and so on.

Another schedule, mainly used with younger children, includes what is referred to as a "2-2-3" schedule. In this arrangement, the children are in the care of one parent for two days, then switch to the other parent's care for two days, and then transfer back to the first parent for three days. This 2-2-3 schedule repeats, beginning with the other parent, and ultimately provides the children with an alternating number of weekdays, and every other weekend with each parent. In addition to the main parenting or custodial schedule, the court will also impose a holiday schedule, extended time to each parent during the summer months, and any additional term that the court may deem appropriate to the family at issue.

A court may order any combination of legal and physical custody that is determined to be in the best interests of the children. Depending on the co-parenting relationship of the parents and other factors presented, the court will always attempt to fashion a parenting arrangement that it deems appropriate to foster the children's needs. In extreme cases, the court may award supervised visitation to one parent in order to protect the interests of the children and/or set a predetermined neutral location for custodial exchanges. If you are concerned either about the safety of your children while they are in the care of your spouse, or concerned about your own safety, please relay these concerns to your attorney during your initial consultation. Note, however, that petitioning a court to take extreme measures to protect the safety of a child is a serious undertaking, and should only be done in good faith. It may require that your attorney hire an expert witness, ask the court to order a formal custody evaluation, or several other actions that he or she might deem necessary to assist the court in making a proper determination. On the other hand, if it is discovered that certain allegations were not made in good faith, the court's wrath may prove disastrous — for both the attorney and for his or her client.

## *Factors Courts Consider*

In order to determine what is in the best interests of a child, most jurisdictions provide enumerated factors that a court must consider when handling custodial issues related to minor children. A jurisdiction may include more or less factors than are included here. The factors include: the age and physical condition of the children; the age and physical and mental condition of the parties; the children's developmental needs; the existing relationship between the children and each parent; the role each parent has played in the children's upbringing; the propensity of a parent to foster the relationship between the children and the other parent; the relationship between the children and other important individuals in his or her life, such as siblings, extended family members, peers, etc.; the children's preferences; any history of family abuse; and finally, any other factor that the court may deem necessary in making an informed decision.

What the foregoing should highlight is that the court does the best it can with the information provided. In most cases, the judge does not personally meet the children who are the subject of the litigation. He or she has no insight into the life of the family, other than what can be expressed in a few words of testimony from the parents and a handful of witnesses. Accordingly, the decision-making burden placed on the court should make it abundantly clear to those involved that this is not a wise parenting option and should be avoided whenever possible. During the marriage, most parents interview childcare providers, schools, tutors, and are scrupulous in their decision-making when it comes to their children's well-being.

However, once they are placed into the divorce process, parents tend to surrender all parenting decisions to the court system as if they have lost the ability to confer and practice parenting together throughout the chaos. Instead, they tend to dig their feet into the sand, or stand firmly on their side of the litigation line and assume a "fighter's stance" as it relates to the new reality for their children. Absent extreme circumstances, there is no rational basis for parents to think that, because they are terminating their marriage vows, their co-parenting relationship must also end.

We understand that children, even during their parents' divorce, do not experience events in terms of right and wrong, or believe that one parent is more worthy of love than the other. However, parents truly struggle with the need to separate the divorce process into two distinct categories.

On the one hand, the divorce will lead to each party living their own individual life. On the other hand, the role of parenting and the family that existed prior to the divorce will remain for a lifetime. There will always be two parents, and the child or children, who make-up the family. The family unit is not dissolved in the divorce process. As uncomfortable as it is to accept this reality, from a child's point of view, whether a parent is married or divorced, living together or separately, "mom" will always be "mom," and "dad" will always be "dad." It is imperative that divorcing parties are reminded of this reality throughout the divorce process.

If the parents believed during the marriage that conflict between them should never be displayed in front of their children, and that they should always present a united front in their parenting style, then it stands to reason that parents going through the divorce process should not have to lose this consistency and value system simply because they are no longer united as a married couple.

The children with parents who firmly embrace this reality and behave in accordance with its underlying principles will thrive, despite the disruption caused by their parents' divorce. There is no substitute for responsible co-parenting decisions made by the two people who best know both the children and the unique needs of the family. It is understandably difficult for parents to work together, at the same time they are separating their intertwined lives; however, the children do not understand why the co-parenting of their parents comes to an abrupt halt simply because the adults in their life are in a dispute.

## *Guardian ad litem*

Upon request of a party, in some jurisdictions, a court has the power to appoint a Guardian *ad litem* to assist in the custody determination. The Guardian *ad litem*, which may be labeled differently in your jurisdiction, serves as the voice of the children. The Guardian *ad litem* will interview the children and the parents. He or she will visit the residence, or any proposed residence of the children, and will speak to school personnel and any other professionals in the children's life deemed pertinent to the case. Once the evaluation is completed, the Guardian *ad litem* will make a formal recommendation to the court. Although the recommendation of a Guardian *ad litem* is not binding on a court's determination, the judge is very likely to fashion a custody arrangement in accordance with the recommendation provided. The additional information the Guardian *ad litem* receives provides a judge with valuable insight on the family circumstances; however, the parties, the children, and all of the professionals interviewed by the Guardian *ad litem* will be keenly aware that a divorce is in process. Thus, the Guardian *ad litem* must read between the lines and use his or her best judgment when making a final recommendation.

The payment of the Guardian *ad litem's* fees will be determined by the court. The court may order that the fees are to be equally shared by the parties, to be paid in different percentages by the parties, or that one party shall be responsible for paying the fees without a contribution from the other party.

## *Formal Custody Evaluation*

A court may order a formal custody evaluation from a mental health professional. The fees for a typical child custody evaluation can cost several thousand dollars. As with the Guardian *ad litem*, the court will also decide how the mental health professional's fees will be paid. The mental health professional, usually a psychologist, will conduct several interviews with both divorcing parties and each child. They will want to observe each child interacting with each parent on more than one occasion. The mental health professional may interview school personnel, therapists, daycare providers and extended family members as a part of their evaluation process.

In more complicated situations, the mental health professional may conduct psychological testing to assist them further in making a sound recommendation. There are circumstances in which a mental health professional will share his or her findings and recommendations with the parties and their attorneys prior to providing them to the court. The purpose of this disclosure is to provide the parties with information that may serve to encourage them to come to an agreement and forego further court determination. As with the Guardian *ad litem*, if the matter proceeds to court, the court will likely fashion a custody arrangement that reflects in large part the recommendations of the mental health professional.

### *Words of Wisdom*

It is important to always be honest with the Guardian *ad litem* or the mental health professional who has been ordered or retained to conduct a custody evaluation. You are advised, of course, to always speak with your attorney; however, most will agree that when engaged in a custody evaluation, you want to highlight the strengths as well as the weaknesses of both parents. Considering that we can all use improvement in one area or another when it comes to our parenting skills, a party who is only capable of pointing fingers at his or her co-parent will appear disingenuous. It is important that a party be able to discuss his or her own shortcomings, as well as what they believe to be the shortcomings of their co-parent, with neutrality, and to compliment and highlight areas in which each party excels.

Keep in mind that Guardians *ad litem* and mental health professionals are charged with the same standard as used by the court, the best interests of the children, when making a recommendation. Thus, it is important to be open to hearing new ideas and to learning why a proposed idea would be in the best interests of the children. It is natural to evaluate an idea in the midst of a custody dispute in terms of how the operation of a proposed idea would personally affect a party; however, it is important to show flexibility and a willingness to do what is in the best interests of the children, even when a more personally convenient approach is available.

I want to be clear that showing good judgment, flexibility, and a willingness to make hard choices while engaging in a custody evaluation process does not mean that you should not also express why you feel an alternative idea would be better suited for your family, and how the proposed idea might impact you personally. I am simply suggesting that an inflexible party with a hard position on custody matters may not create the best rapport with the Guardian *ad litem* or the mental health professional. If the Guardian *ad litem* or the mental health professional believes that either party is using the children as a means of hurting the other party, be it consciously or unconsciously, the child custody factor shared earlier concerning a parent's willingness or ability to foster the relationship of the children with the other parent will be critically lacking, and could lead to a unfavorable result in terms of the final recommendation.

Accordingly, be yourself, be honest, encourage your children to be honest, and allow the party making the recommendation to trust that you will always do what is in the best interests of your children. A trained Guardian *ad litem* or a mental health professional understands that you are in the middle of a major life transition; however, they also understand that raising children comes with many moments of uncertainty and requires a parent to be consistent in their ability to make good decisions, even when life throws them a curveball. The midst of the divorce chaos is the perfect backdrop for a professional to evaluate a party's parenting skills under pressure. It is natural to feel vulnerable during this process; however, engaging from a place of integrity will be your strongest weapon.

Unless the possibility of reaching an amicable custodial arrangement out of court is hopeless due to an abusive or other extreme circumstance, in most cases there is no one more capable of co-creating a parenting plan than your co-parent. There are many resources and professionals available to assist in the process. A good start is to remember the concept that your family will always be a family; it will just look different than it once did. This simple acknowledgment will help both parents maintain their perspective, and will foster behaviors that are more likely to engender safety, security and wholeness in the lives of their innocent children who are also experiencing, and will be affected by, their parents' divorce. Our main role as parents is to provide nurturing that allows children to blossom, to be children, and to experience life as children, without the burdens of adult trials and tribulations.

## *Retaining a Mental Health Professional*

There are times when the parties desire to settle issues related to their children outside of the court process, and may choose to retain the services of a mental health professional to assist them and their attorneys in reaching a custody arrangement. In such cases, the parties will view the mental health professional as a neutral resource, and will make an agreement in advance to cooperate with this expert and to make his or her recommendations a priority in settlement discussions. Whether the mental health professional may be called as an expert at trial, in the event the parties are unable to reach an amicable settlement, is a discussion you must have with your attorney prior to engaging in the process. Typically, the parties will agree that the mental health professional may not be called as an expert at trial by either party without the written consent of the other party.

However, it is important to understand how the confidentiality rules apply to settlement discussions and to neutral, retained experts who are used during the settlement process, so that you are clear on how the information they gather can be used, and to what extent. It is highly recommended that you consider this option if decisions concerning the custody of your children are in dispute.

Your attorney will provide recommendations for respected mental health professionals with whom they have worked in previous cases. You and your spouse should have the opportunity to meet with more than one professional, and thereafter make a joint decision on which professional will be hired to work with you and your attorneys. The act of meeting jointly with a mental health professional who is there to assist you and your spouse in making the best decisions concerning the well-being of your children, and who can make recommendations for the specific nuances that are unique to your family, should naturally lead to a feeling of comfort.

The mental health professional will proceed in a similar fashion, as was noted in the previous section; however, rather than the experience being laced with fear about the likely result, with the right professional, the expert becomes a partner in the process. The mental health professional may, in certain cases, become an ongoing resource for the family following the divorce process as the children grow up and circumstances change.

From my experience, having the right mental health professional working with the parties and the attorneys early in the divorce process not only aids in informed decision-making, but also serves to fortify the concept that a family in transition remains a family. With that understanding, parents learn to master new communication skills, to appreciate the other parent's role in the life of the children, and to co-parent more naturally and respectfully. Most importantly, the needs of the children are nurtured, which allows them to blossom — despite the harsh reality of their parents' divorce.

# 5

# Financial Support for Children and Child Support

In every jurisdiction, both parents have a responsibility for the financial support of their children. When parents are married or partnered together, the children are considered children of the marriage or partnership. This means that the support needs of the children are presumably met within that union. However, in the event of a separation and/or divorce, absent an agreement by the parents, the support needs of minor children will be addressed by the court in the form of a separate child support order, or within the divorce decree. A common misconception of parents receiving support is that the amount awarded should cover all the expenses which that parent needs to raise the children.

It is important to understand that a child support award is to serve as an equitable contribution toward the expenses paid by the custodial parent for housing, food, clothing, school expenses, extracurricular activities, and other related child expenses; it is not, however, designed to cover the entirety of these expenses. As soon as this concept is understood, the issue of child support becomes less of a mystery. In the next section, we will discuss the methods used by the court to determine a child support award, and how such support is determined when the parents have a shared or split-custody arrangement.

## *Child Support Guidelines*

Historically, child support was awarded by courts on a case-by-case basis, and each state was unique in how it determined child support in its jurisdiction. Whether a jurisdiction used the budgets of the parents to establish a support amount, a list of factors, the unique characteristics of the family, or a combination of the above, the awards were inconsistent. Congress passed the Child Support Enforcement Amendments of 1984 [Pub. L. No. 93-647, 88 Stat 2337 (codified at 42 U.S.C. §§ 651-662 (1988)], which mandated the states to adopt child support guidelines. Subsequent regulations mandated that the guidelines shall be in the form of a predictable mathematical formula, and that the application of the guidelines shall carry a rebuttable presumption that the result is the correct child support amount to be awarded. A rebuttable presumption means that the court must view the guideline as the appropriate amount of child support in the case at issue; however, a judge may use his or her discretion to deviate from the guideline amount of child support, if he or she finds evidence to deem it appropriate. One can argue that, if a court has the right to ignore the guidelines and deviate from the guideline amount, child support awards remain inconsistent; however, the burden is on the party requesting a deviation to convince the court that the guideline amount is inappropriate, and that his or her proposed deviation would yield a more equitable result.

Most jurisdictions require that the guideline amount of child support be noted in a child support order or divorce decree, and the justification for the court's deviation also be explained. The use of standard guidelines is an asset during settlement discussions and provides the attorneys with a ballpark figure when advising their clients about what can be expected in terms of court-ordered child support.

To create a guideline that accurately reflects an appropriate amount of support in a particular location, each state creates a baseline from which other factors are considered. Thus, economic factors — such as the labor market, average earnings, unemployment rates, the federal poverty level, and other factors — are utilized in determining a baseline for the guideline formula. If the cost-of-living deviates drastically from one location to another, a state may institute area-specific guidelines. The baseline is then used to calculate the child support amount from the individual factors relevant to each case.

Although each jurisdiction may vary, the individual factors that are inputted into the guidelines for the purpose of calculating child support typically include some combination of the following: the earnings and income of the non-custodial parent, or both parents; income that has been imputed to a parent due to voluntary unemployment or underemployment (meaning that the income that is factored into the guideline for that parent will be the income the court determines they could be earning based upon the evidence presented); the number of children; spousal support payable by one party to the other, if any; the premium paid by a party to maintain the children as dependents on his or her health insurance policy (the delta between self-only coverage and dependent coverage); and, work-related childcare expenses.

Other factors a court may consider when determining whether the guideline child support amount is appropriate in a particular case might include: debts incurred by either party on behalf of a child; special needs of a child; payments a party is ordered to pay for the education, tuition, or other specific benefits on behalf of a child; independent income a child might receive; tax benefits or consequences to either party; any ongoing extraordinary medical expenses; other dependents living in the home of either party; and, a previous court-ordered child support obligation for any children not born of the parties' union. The standard of living a child enjoyed during the marriage is also considered.

In the case of a shared-custody arrangement, where both parents' custodial time with the children is roughly equal, or when a non-custodial parent's visitation time exceeds a certain number of days-per-year, many states use a shared-custody guideline to accommodate these circumstances. In the case of split-custody, whereby each parent is awarded custody of at least one child, a child support guideline is used for each child, and the sums are offset against each other. Unless the sums are equal, the parent who owes the greater amount will have a child support obligation payable to the other parent. Finally, many states simply treat shared or split custody arrangements as a deviation from a standard guideline calculation.

## Child Support Guideline Models

There are three basic child support guideline models used in the United States. The first is known as the Flat Percentage Model. The factors inputted into this model include the payor's income and the number of children to be supported. The second model, which is used most, is known as the Income Shares Model. The factors inputted into the calculation of this model include the income of both parties, the number of children to be supported, health insurance premium cost, work-related daycare expenses, and in some jurisdictions, education expenses. The third model is known as the Melson Formula Model. This model is like the Income Shares Model, but also includes an adjustment for the standard of living as a part of the guideline calculation. Your attorney will advise you on the appropriate child support guideline and any common deviations in your jurisdiction.

## Uninsured and Unreimbursed Medical Expenses

Expenses related to uninsured or unreimbursed medical expenses such as co-pays and deductibles are no longer considered in the basic child support guidelines. These expenses are treated separately as an add-on, or as a deviation to the guideline child support amount. A jurisdiction may order these expenses paid by the parties in proportion to their income shares, or they may set a threshold amount per year, per child, that must be exceeded by the party receiving child support before receiving a contribution from the other parent.

## Child Support Arrangements by Agreement

It is very common for parents to reach an out-of-court agreement concerning the support of their children. In many of these cases, the parents create their own child support arrangements which do not follow the structure of the guidelines. They may each agree to pay for certain expenses individually, or they may share certain expenses in pre-determined percentages. There may or may not be a payment from one parent to the other. In most jurisdictions, an agreement concerning child support is honored and will be sanctioned by the court. However, the court has the power to either accept or reject an agreed-upon child support arrangement. It is important to note that child support is a support right belonging to the child. Therefore, a parent cannot waive a child's right to receive financial support by agreement, and any clause in an agreement purporting to waive such a right to support may be deemed invalid if later challenged.

In the following section, we will discuss the duration of a child support obligation, and what happens in the event of a change of circumstances prior to emancipation.

## Duration of Child Support

Once child support has been established, the obligation will continue until a child is considered "emancipated." In most states, emancipation occurs when a child reaches the age of eighteen years, provided they have also graduated from high school. If a child has not graduated from high school by the age of eighteen, then the child support obligation will continue until such time as the child either graduates from high school or reaches the age of nineteen years, whichever occurs first. There are a few jurisdictions that define a child's emancipation for child support purposes at age twenty or above, depending on certain circumstances. Moreover, most jurisdictions will extend a child support obligation past the age of emancipation for a child who is mentally or physically disabled and also living in the home of the parent receiving support. Finally, a child support obligation may terminate early if the child marries, joins the military, or otherwise becomes self-supporting prior to emancipation.

## *When Circumstances Change*

Once a child support obligation is in place, circumstances existing at the time of the child support award may change. In the event of a change of circumstances that affects a child's support rights, either parent may petition the court for a modification. Some common circumstances that may motivate a parent to request a modification may include: the loss of employment; a decrease of income or an increase in the other parent's income; a parent incurring expenses unforeseeable at the time of the initial award; or, one of the children named in the child support order has reached the age of emancipation or has otherwise triggered an emancipation event, which would be considered a change of circumstances.

However, it is important to note that, other than a change of circumstances dealing with an emancipation event, in order to successfully modify a current child support order, most jurisdictions require that the change also be material. The term "material," however, is rather subjective. What may appear to be material to a parent living with the change of circumstances may not be considered sufficiently material to the court to justify a modification to the current child support award. Therefore, it is important to discuss with your attorney any potential future changes that you foresee prior to the entry of a child support award.

The above discussion is a broad overview of how the issue of child support is treated in different jurisdictions. Just as with other issues incident to your divorce, it is important that you consult with an attorney in your jurisdiction so that you know how child support will be determined, and what options may be available to you.

# 6

# Choosing Your Attorney

One of the most important decisions you will make on your divorce journey is choosing the attorney who will be walking beside you. Your attorney will represent your interests in all phases of the divorce, and will become your partner throughout the process. Therefore, there are four main factors to consider when choosing an attorney.

First, does the attorney have the qualifications to provide you with sound and responsible representation? Your attorney should be experienced in family law, and have a concentration, or at least a strong emphasis, in divorce. You will want to learn how long the attorney has been representing divorcing clients; however, keep in mind that a longer or shorter practice history does not always indicate the quality of representation you will receive. It is good information to have, but only one factor to consider. You will want to learn if he or she is familiar with the divorce laws in your state as well as with the unique rules of court in your jurisdiction. The courts in each state, from one city or county to the next, may have their own culture, distinct procedural rules, and expectations of the attorneys who practice in their courthouse. During an initial consultation, an experienced attorney will usually speak of the "norms" of the court or courts in which they practice. Understanding the "culture" of the court, the attorney is better suited to develop a strategy tailored to your situation.

Second, it is important to get a sense of the attorney's reputation in the legal community. Depending on the process you choose for your divorce, be it traditional litigation, traditional negotiation, the collaborative process, or mediation, it is key that you choose an attorney best suited for that process. You may not know which process you will choose in the beginning; however, be sure that the attorney and the process chosen are a good fit, prior to fully engaging the attorney to work with you. I do not mean to imply that a good litigator cannot also successfully represent your interests in an alternative process, or vice-versa; however, there are relevant distinctions in the way an attorney operates, depending on the process. As with any profession, most attorneys naturally gravitate to the process that best reflects their personality and preferences.

Remember, attorneys are human beings. They not only have experience in their field, but they also have personal biases, beliefs, preferences, reputations, and certain known standards of behavior. If an attorney has been referred to you based on that attorney's performance in a traditional litigation case, it is important to know how they get along with others, their court decorum, are they respected by other members in the community, or if other attorneys work with them with a bit of chagrin. Do they have a reputation for truthfulness? Do they honor their word? Do they operate from a place of integrity, or are they focused on the "win," notwithstanding the rules of engagement, the integrity of the profession, or even their client's integrity?

On the surface, a person may feel safe in the hands of an attorney who proudly sports the reputation of a "bulldog" in the community; however, it is important to ask yourself if you would be comfortable bringing such a person to every occasion. There are certainly times when a case is hotly contested, and an attorney with this personality and skill might be necessary to protect a party's interests. Moreover, if one party retains an attorney who fits this description, the other party might feel the need for an appropriate counterpart to balance the playing field. However, in these situations, the parties may each be subject to the complete surrender of control over the process.

Like other professions, many attorneys talk about each other and make referrals to each other; it is a natural part of the profession. There are attorneys who at first glance appear to be leaders in their community. The question is not always whether they are a leader; the true inquiry is how they achieved that leadership reputation, and what that leadership role means in terms of your case. As with any area of life, a true leader is one who operates with the highest level of integrity, a full understanding of their field of practice, gets along well with others, and can be competitive, while at the same time demonstrating dignity and respect. An attorney who has the reputation of being an honest player, pleasant to work with, and respected in the community, will not only represent your interests well in the divorce, but will also likely do so with a focus on minimizing cost, both financially and emotionally. He or she can remain neutral and balanced in their decorum, while representing your interests fully. Most importantly, an attorney with this make-up will never lose sight of the fact that your family is the focus of the process — a family with emotions and real lives to live. A family's financial future, the well-being of each of the parties and their children, and many other issues are intimate and personal. Responsible and proper legal counsel and judgment throughout the process is crucial.

Third, in addition to having the qualifications that will provide you with solid and responsible representation, there must also be a harmony between your energy and the energy of the attorney you choose to work with. It is important to assess certain personal characteristics of the attorney. Pay attention to how you feel in their presence. Ask yourself if you feel comfortable in his or her office, and with the office staff. Do you feel comfortable expressing yourself to the attorney? Do you feel the attorney is fully listening to you, or do they appear distracted? Do you feel anxious, shameful, or any other unpleasant emotion? Is the attorney focusing on the facts you present and developing an immediate plan, or is he or she encouraging you to discuss your unique needs, desires, fears, and perhaps even your vision for the future? In other words, does the attorney appear to have a genuine interest in you and your family? Do you feel as though the attorney will be accessible to you, answer your questions, and provide you with the level of personal attention you feel you will need during the process? Some clients require more communication with their attorney during the process than others. It is important that you feel your needs will be met.

Fourth, when choosing an attorney, make sure that he or she is forthright with you concerning your expectations. Based upon the facts and circumstances of your case, are your expectations within the realm of fairness, or do they exceed the boundaries of what can be expected in a case such as yours? When you hear stories about another individual's divorce, remember that each case is different, and that the dynamics of each family are unique. A story that ends with a victory in litigation does not describe the emotional and financial cost to the family involved. Sometimes, upon a closer examination of all the facts of a particular case, the "win" may not be such a "win" after all. When you take a seat in an attorney's office, use your intuition, along with the information above, to decide if the attorney is a good fit for you and your family.

If you receive advice from your attorney to do, say, or agree to something that does not resonate with you, pay attention. That part of you that says, "this is not right for me," must be honored. Too often, parties do not speak up honestly to let their attorneys know what is truly important to them. Perhaps a thought you shared two weeks ago is no longer important or relevant. As you proceed through your case, frequently practice tuning in to yourself — be it through meditation, a walk in nature, or simply five minutes of quiet contemplation — and ask from that deep place within you, questions such as, "Where am I now? What is important to me now? What have I said or agreed to? Do these concepts still hold truth for me?" It is not a sign of weakness to want to pivot midstream and to speak up, to speak your truth, even if that is in direct conflict with your initial thoughts.

Your divorce case is not a time to worry about what others think of you, particularly family, friends, colleagues, or anyone else outside the case. Divorce will be very personal to you, your spouse, and your children; it should be treated that way. The more information a party receives from outside sources — and sometimes this even includes one's own attorney — the more likely it is that a decision will be made from a place other than from that party's truth. A walk in integrity has many sides. It is important to maintain your integrity throughout the process. This means listening to that voice within you that knows the bigger picture. You must look to your own compass for guidance. Always follow your own integrity of what is right and wrong. When a party participates in their divorce from a place of integrity, their focus becomes clear and they are better able to define their needs. Any fear they experience can be quieted enough so that they are able to listen and speak from their heart, rather than from their ego mind. Even when you mistrust your spouse, always take the time to honor and have trust in yourself. You are always the best judge of your own requirements, and those of your family. A process that respects this truth will best serve you long-term.

# PART I [B]

# The Four Processes of Divorce

In this section, we will discuss the four processes available in the handling of your divorce. We will start with a candid discussion about the traditional litigation process. To make the information easier to understand, we will be using the metaphor of a stage play when covering this topic. We will then move on to a discussion of the mediation process, followed by the collaborative process; and finally, we will discuss the option of a self-negotiated/hybrid process.

# 7

# The Traditional Litigation Process In-Depth Preview

To set up our stage play metaphor, we can think of the courthouse as the theater venue where the stage play will be performed. The divorcing parties and their witnesses will take on the roles of stage actors. The attorneys, as agents and stage managers, will represent the divorcing parties; however, they will also have performing roles in the play. Moreover, the attorneys will be responsible for weaving together the story line and creating the plots that will be presented. The judge will serve as the audience, the director of the play while it is in process, and the all-important role of critic.

The attorneys will zealously represent their individual clients and do all that they can within the rules of a particular jurisdiction to achieve the outcomes desired by their clients. It is important to emphasize that litigation involves two opposing positions on most issues. Experiencing the adversarial process of advocating two opposing positions, and not knowing the outcome until the last act of the stage play, naturally engenders fear in the litigating spouses. Whenever we are fearful, our natural instincts and ego step in to protect us from harm and promote our survival.

Just like writers of the stage play, attorneys create a theme for each case. Each attorney's opposing theme of the case is created from the representations they receive from their clients and from the supporting evidence they can gather. It is important to note that the clients' desired outcomes play critical roles in the creation and tone of the themes to be presented. Weaving a story together is only one step. The story must be presented credibly and supported by sound evidence if the judge, as the critic, is going to be moved enough to make a ruling in the client's favor.

As an example, if a client desires to be credited with a separate interest in a particular asset, their attorney will be looking for documentation and any other form of evidence that would support the separate interest claim. Under this example, there is no need to dig deeper than the paper trail. However, the situation changes if the client desires to receive a larger percentage of a particular asset because he or she believes it would be a more equitable outcome, based upon the circumstances of their marriage. The attorney will now need sufficient evidence that a claim of more than half of the value of the asset is appropriate. To do this, in many cases, the client will be asked to pull out every fact from the past they can in order to support their contention that their spouse should receive less. Thus, the attorney will need to highlight the shadow side of their client's spouse. Commonly referred to as "dirty laundry" evidence, this includes emphasizing negative actions or inaction of the spouse, which might convince a judge to rule in the client's favor.

When too much attention is allocated to this negatively charged process, it unfortunately tends to undermine and cloud the judgment of each party — becoming a tangled web of "who said what? who did what?" The process can obscure what is truly important to the former marriage partners and to their children, as well as their sense of right and wrong. Accordingly, a party desiring a disparate share of the marital assets must be careful not to get lost down a rabbit hole, dredging up the shadows of their spouse to the point that they lose sight of the light side of their spouse, as well as the light side within themselves. Any remaining trust that may have been present between the parties can be irretrievably lost. With both sides searching for evidence to defend against "dirty laundry allegations" made by the other, while at the same time searching for evidence to support their own theory of the case, this negative energy naturally gains a downward-spiraling momentum.

It is important to note that an attorney, based upon experience, will advise his or her client to take certain actions to protect themselves, and will warn them of certain actions in which their spouse may engage. While this is a necessary discussion intended to protect a client's interests, it can and does result in accentuating fear and raising uncertainty. One or both of the parties may engage in nefarious conduct during the process. Example: A party might withdraw all the funds from their joint account, out of fear that the other party might do that first. This type of behavior by one or both of the parties serves to perpetuate and intensify the adversarial nature of the process. As a pre-emptive tool, the parties and their attorneys may agree to equally divide a joint account or suspend use of the account either until an agreement is reached, or a court determination is made.

Keep in mind that there are individuals who acted with integrity during the marriage and will maintain that integrity despite what the other side might do during the divorce. There are also individuals who acted with integrity during the marriage, but who can be persuaded to step outside of their integrity when they are embroiled in an adversarial process. Accordingly, it is important to use your own discernment as it relates to any steps you might take, affirmatively or defensively, during this time.

When the custody of children is part of the litigation, the parties can lose sight of the most important truth — that the dissolution of their marriage does not dissolve the family; the family simply transforms. However, when parents find themselves in an adversarial system centered upon winning and losing, the potential for a successful transition of the family from one household to a healthy and functioning two-home arrangement for the children can easily be destroyed. By its very nature, litigation morphs into a game of winning and losing. The parents are almost helpless against a process that has the power to provide a win to one party by deciding that he or she is the preferred or fit custodial parent, while taking away or limiting the other party's parenting time. It is only natural that a parent will fight hard and long to maintain his or her role as the primary parent of their children.

### Formal Discovery

Using our analogy of the stage play, the parties to the divorce, their witnesses, and any expert witnesses who will be offering testimony, must be groomed for their role. Months of effort go into preparing testimony and gathering and organizing evidence that will be presented at trial. In addition to the information and documentation the attorneys receive from their own clients, attorneys use a formal discovery process to gather evidence from the opposing party and other sources. As the name implies, it is a procedural process allowing an attorney to "discover" information which might lead to evidence relevant to the case.

The discovery process in each jurisdiction may have slightly different rules the attorney must observe; however, the process uniformly includes several tools for obtaining information. One such tool is the use of Interrogatories — a set of written questions an attorney asks the other party to answer under oath. Another tool available in the discovery process is a Request for Documents — allowing the attorney to compel the other party to produce certain documents. An attorney can also ask the other party to admit or deny in writing certain statements, under oath, in a document known as a Request for Admissions. An attorney can also take the deposition of the other party or their witnesses — allowing the attorney to ask questions of those parties directly, in real-time, and under oath. In addition to seeking evidence in a deposition, a deposition often serves as a quasi-dress rehearsal, giving the attorney a preview to gauge the credibility of the opposing party and their witnesses and how effectively they will perform their roles on the witness stand at trial. Finally, a tool known as a subpoena *duces tecum* can be used to compel documents from third-party organizations and witnesses.

The discovery process is often highly contentious. There are many valid reasons why an attorney may object to his or her client answering a question or producing a requested document. At times, a party might refuse a request, despite the advice of his or her counsel. If the parties cannot agree on a resolution, the attorney for the party requesting the information will schedule a discovery hearing and ask the court to settle the dispute. At times, both parties might have discovery objections pending before the court. The court might affirm the objection and rule that the objecting party does not have to comply with the discovery, or the court might overrule the objection and order compliance.

If you are beginning to feel a hole developing in your pocket or handbag, you would be right. The formal discovery process is a very expensive proposition. It is important to pause here for a moment to note that, once litigation has begun, it is each attorney's affirmative responsibility to engage in the discovery process to receive what he or she needs to present their client's case. Attorneys are ethically bound to represent their clients zealously; therefore, they cannot run the risk of breaching this duty by failing to engage in the discovery process in hopes that the case will settle prior to trial.

When the attorneys are searching for evidence that supports their clients' desire for custody, they are looking for specific evidence relating to the statutory factors a judge must use in making a custody determination. Thus, attorneys are focusing their attention on discovering evidence that will convince the court that his or her client is the more suited or fit parent, while simultaneously highlighting the shortcomings of the other party. Whereas the discovery process is a search for objective evidence when dealing with an easily measurable asset, such as a bank account, evidence related to child custody is mainly subjective in nature and therefore much more difficult to develop. One area of a court's subjective inquiry is the parenting arrangement during the marriage. This includes the daily responsibilities for feeding and caring for the children, providing homework assistance, attending school conferences and doctor's appointments, providing transportation to and from school and/or extracurricular activities, as well as spending quality time with the children when school is not in session.

If you notice that your spouse has begun engaging in activities with the children that seem uncharacteristic to previously established patterns, it may be that your spouse has been advised to step-up their parenting role in order to more positively impact a judge's custody determination. When this happens, the primary parent usually begins taking countermeasures. This results in parents working against each other, rather than in concert for the children's best interests. In addition, the parties may begin disingenuously enlisting doctors, teachers, counselors, coaches, and other adults connected to the children's lives as potential witnesses to their custodial fitness. The relationship between the children and these adults naturally becomes strained and uncomfortable. Unfortunately, a party cannot proceed with a custody trial without sufficient evidence to support their request for primary custody. Mutual character assassination of the parents is, unfortunately, common in this process and cannot be reversed. Whatever light existed in the parenting relationship prior to a custody trial is now severely dimmed, if not extinguished.

In addition to the discovery process, a litigated case may also include one or more temporary hearings dealing with living arrangements, temporary support and/or custody arrangements. Without an agreement of the parties, the court will enter temporary orders that will be in place until the final determination of these matters. Moreover, some jurisdictions will determine child custody matters in a trial or hearing separate from the trial on the issues of property distribution, support matters, and the grounds for divorce.

It is important to take a minute and "feel into" the discovery process just described. Even during those times when there are no discovery responses pending, hearings to prepare for and attend, and other case-related matters, the mind is in a continual state of unrest. The parties can become trapped in a place of fear and their minds may be flooded with questions, such as, "What will happen if this or that should take place? What will I do? Will I be OK? What will become of me? How will I get past this? What about my children?" It is common for a party in litigation to be so consumed with uncertainly that his or her mind begins to conjure up fear-based, self-created prophesies that become the focus and the backdrop from which each decision is made thereafter. Soon, whatever trust they had in themselves is overshadowed; whatever inner knowing they had concerning the goodness, integrity, or compassion of their spouse is forgotten — swallowed up and absorbed into an endless sea of doubt, disdain, mistrust, and misunderstanding.

## *Settlement Proposals During Litigation*

Most divorce litigation cases include at least one written settlement proposal exchange, or one or more settlement conferences attended by the parties and their attorneys. Although many settlement discussions take place early in the process, too many parties experience the less-desirable alternative of receiving a settlement proposal from their spouse's attorney very close to trial — sometimes on the eve of trial. It is not a stretch to imagine the mindset and lack of clarity each of the parties are experiencing, while at the same time being asked to "settle" or "compromise" or "do the right thing" — as if they were able to determine what the "right thing" might be under these conditions. At times, a party takes advantage of knowing that the other party is fearful of going to trial and, accordingly, presents a lopsided, less-than-favorable settlement as an alternative.

In most cases, a thoughtful attorney will recommend that his or her client propose a settlement offer early in the process — that is, if they have enough information to assist their client in doing so. As an example, if the discovery process has not produced enough evidence of a party's income, making a settlement offer on the issue of spousal or child support would be premature. Divorcing parties naturally become confused when they have spent months preparing their case for trial, and their attorney suddenly recommends that they propose a settlement offer. There are many reasons that might justify this recommendation. A mindful attorney might realize that the case is beginning to exceed the client's emotional capacity, or that the client's case is weak, based upon the evidence gathered. Rather than risk an unfavorable result at trial, the attorney might suggest that the client settle on agreed-upon terms, in lieu of waiting for a court's determination.

In any event, once litigation is in full swing and trial is near, a settlement reached under this type of pressure is one made in fear and exhaustion, rather than from a place of creatively designing a settlement that is durable, long-lasting, and meets the needs of the family. It is rare that divorcing parties are content with a settlement reached under these circumstances. They may be relieved that the process is over, but most will admit that the terms of the settlement were not tailored to their best interests, or the best interests of their family.

## *The Trial*

If settlement negotiations fail, the play must still go on. It is time for each party and their witnesses to put on their best performance. The many months of preparation, script changes and rehearsal come down to this one opportunity to shine. The attorneys each take turns presenting their theory of the case. Each client's testimony is crafted to project their perception of the marriage. Depending on the issues in dispute, one spouse's testimony might consist of their account of what caused the dissolution of the marriage — who did or did not do what, who said what, who should receive more, who should receive less, who was the better parent, who is more deserving or undeserving, who can be trusted and who is not to be trusted, and so on.

The opposing party's attorney can then attempt to discredit this testimony by cross-examining them. Most readers have witnessed a cross-examination on a television drama or movie screen; although these performances are scripted dramatically at the expense of real trial proceedings, they do portray the unflattering and disrespectful nature of the process. During a party's presentation of their theory of the case, the party's witnesses will also make cameo appearances on the court's stage to provide corroborating and supporting evidence. These witnesses will also face cross-examination from the opposing party's counsel. The testimony provided by the parties and their witnesses, as well as any documentary evidence presented by either party, will be admitted or denied by our drama critic — the sitting judge.

Just like a theatre critic, it is in the light of this one performance that the judge will render his or her own opinion. The judge is charged with making lasting rulings on the issues brought before the court, based upon an extremely limited and distorted snapshot of the marriage. This is not a criticism of family court judges. However, the important nuances of the family, the needs and desires of the parties and the children are, sadly, lost in the procedural carving up of relevant and admissible evidence. A family's most intimate and sacred experiences are exposed and judged and regarded or disregarded. Assumptions concerning a party's credibility must be made from the limited testimony presented under these less-than-ideal conditions.

Where the focus is on winning, this naturally means that someone must lose. One spouse and his or her witnesses must be found to be more credible than the other spouse and his or her witnesses. From this one performance, many years of the lives of each party, and the lives of the parties' children and other important family members, will be affected. Even a spouse who experiences an apparent "win" in the litigation will naturally experience loss as its counterpart. There is no process that can divide a life union and a marital estate, and simultaneously fairly address each of the decisions made during the marriage concerning employment, financial matters, child-rearing, and other issues unique to a particular family. Attorneys have been known to use the phrase, "You can't split a baby in half." Accordingly, there will always be a need for compromise when it comes to the divorce process. Whether it is a natural byproduct of the litigation process, or inherent in the intentions of the parties as they navigate a resolution by an alternative, less-adversarial process, compromises do and will exist. Acknowledging this truth at the beginning of the process is essential in setting the right tone for the journey.

Many parties are fueled by their need to be heard and validated. The reasons for wanting their case to proceed to trial — even risking the possibility of an undesirable outcome — are born from a place of pain. However, there is often a mistaken belief that a judge will validate their feelings and perceptions if they are just able to "tell their story." This type of misunderstanding of the process only perpetuates a party's fear, and prevents them from making sound decisions. When a judge listens to a party's "story" in the form of their testimony or the testimony of their witnesses, the judge is listening from the standpoint of his or her place on the bench. From that same bench the judge hears many similar stories and fact patterns. Only on those rare occasions when a party's "story" includes an anomaly, such as severe physical, emotional and/ or financial abuse, are the judge's ears truly piqued. It is not that a party's circumstance is unimportant, or that the party does not deserve a caring or sympathetic ear, it is simply one story of many proffered in a judge's courtroom by individuals seeking to dissolve their marriage.

A judge is human; he or she is asked to listen carefully to testimony of past events, review documentary evidence, and, based upon that evidence and the law, is then charged with deciding the pending issues. Unlike a referee at a sporting event who is present in real time and witnessing the players in action before making a judgment call, the sitting judge has not been privy to the sanctity of your private relationship, your conversations, the decisions made during the marriage and the reasons why certain decisions were made, or what caused the marriage to dissolve. No amount of testimony will allow a judge to thoroughly understand the complexity of each marriage. Therefore, it requires a tremendous amount of trust to choose to place decisions of such importance in the hands of a third party — particularly when, as often occurs, both parties are left feeling disappointed and vengeful. If there is only one issue that you and your spouse can agree upon early in the divorce process, this should be the area of focus.

# 8

# Post-Trial

The end of the trial is not always the end of the litigation story. If a party is dissatisfied with a court's ruling, he or she may attempt to appeal one or more of the issues decided. In some cases, both parties may file appeals. However, due to financial concerns and the sheer exhaustion from the trial process, many of the parties in these situations simply accede to the court's ruling. If there is an appeal, the appellate court will either affirm the judge's decision, or will send the issue back to the trial court with instructions. Depending on the issue and the instructions given, the parties may be forced to relitigate the issue, in whole or in part. Although most attorneys will advise against an appeal if the financial and emotional costs to their client will outweigh the potential reward of a second bite at the apple, there are some who will encourage their clients to appeal, if there is the slightest chance the appellate court will overturn the ruling.

Many parties, particularly those receiving unfavorable child custody determinations, will begin strategizing about how they will get the court to modify the ruling before the ink has dried on the paper. It can become a mission of the party who is dissatisfied with a custody order to become hyper-focused on the slightest indiscretion in the other parent's adherence to the court's order. It is not uncommon for clients to ask their attorneys for specific guidance on what they need to do to gear up for the next round of litigation. For these parents, any advice from their attorney to work within the confines of the order falls on deaf ears; they simply cannot hear it. Thus, rather than birthing a healthy co-parenting relationship post-trial, the exhausting negative energy of the trial experience lives on, in an endless loop of litigation. For these individuals, disputes over parenting issues with their co-parent occur often, and the court becomes the default method to resolve them.

In the next section, we will briefly discuss some of the impact the litigation process has on the children of divorcing parents.

## *Impact on Children*

Custodial matters provide the best example of the post-divorce reality of litigation. Rather than the parties choosing to shine with their co-parenting skills and presenting a unified front for the children, they begin looking for examples of why the other parent should not have custodial rights to the children, and/or why the other parent should not be included in legal decisions concerning the children's health, education and welfare. The reality that they will forever have to share their children with the other parent, sometimes without the children in their presence for long periods of time, is heartbreaking and unnatural for most parents. It is a new paradigm for parents to worry about when they will see their children, how decisions concerning their children must now be made, what they may or may not do when the children are in their care, and whether their children are safe in the other parent's care.

A parent who has a hard time adjusting may begin denying scheduled access or visitation to the other parent. He or she may be late for scheduled pick-ups and/or drop-offs. Some parents may fail to inform the other party of a child's health-related matter or tend to be later and later with court-ordered child support payments. A parent may become concerned about a child's adjustment to the constant movement between two homes, two bedrooms, and two disparate home environments, and then look for ways of highlighting the problems rather than working with their co-parent to find workable solutions. A parent may schedule extracurricular activities without the other parent's consent, which interferes with, or perhaps prevents, a parent's scheduled access or visitation with the children.

All day-to-day decisions that were once part of a natural co-parenting experience can become challenged and scrutinized by the other parent. It is common for one or both parents to involve the children by questioning them about what happened, and who was present when they were in the care of the other parent, and they may begin using the children to convey messages to the other parent, rather than communicating directly. The children in these situations are naturally apprehensive about being in the middle. On the one hand, they feel they are at risk of facing punishment from the parent whose information they are disclosing; and, on the other hand, they are at risk of receiving punishment from the parent demanding the information.

Not surprisingly, each real or perceived departure from the terms of a court order by one parent fuels the other parent's fury and provides the ammunition, whether based on sound reasoning or not, to seek further court intervention. In such a hostile environment, it is inevitable that post-divorce motions will be filed with the court to modify custody, to enforce existing custody rulings, and/or to impose sanctions for court order violations.

It is common for a parent with limited resources to feel threatened that their co-parent will "win" a child's love and affection simply because that co-parent has greater resources. Both parents overlook their inner knowing that financial and/or material abundance creates only fleeting moments of satisfaction considering the short attention span of a child. Also ignored is the fact that a child can experience a strong sense of love, safety and belonging even in the most meager of environments. A child experiences his sense of safety and overall well-being from the raw love, nurturing, understanding and connection he receives from his parents. A room full of extraordinary toys nestled in the most luxurious surroundings will have minimal effect on a child's sense of belonging and well-being. In fact, if such an environment is not balanced with a consistent flow of meaningful, one-on-one interactions and proper nurturing from a parent, a child might begin resenting these distractions and become rebellious, or alternately, a child might withdraw into himself. Unable to communicate what he is experiencing on the inside, based on the appearance of such outward behavior, a child soon finds himself labeled as unappreciative, self-centered, or maladjusted.

In the struggle to become the more favored parent, whether through financial purchases, decisions concerning eating habits, bedtimes, or other such attempts to "gain a child's approval," parents can unknowingly create an internal struggle for the child. Children are highly intuitive, and are quite aware of the conscious and sometimes subconscious competition between their "rival" parents; they are simply too young and lack the wisdom to safely navigate their way through this unnatural situation.

You have heard of children engaging in the manipulation of their parents — that enticing game of playing one parent against the other to see how much a child can get away with? The stakes increase dramatically in the situation of a transitioning family, or a family that has completed the transition and is now operating from two independent households. Even older children often lack the tools to make their way through the struggle of competing parents. Except for those situations that involve physical and/or severe emotional abuse, it is not natural for a child of any age to extend favor to one parent over another, to take the side of one parent against the other, or to feel the need to defend one parent against the other.

It is important for divorcing parents to remember that their children are not equipped with the ability to, nor do they want the responsibility to, cast judgment and offer opinions concerning a parent. Children have a natural love and longing for both of their parents. Even in those families where one parent is only marginally involved in a child's life, that child seldom loses their internal connection and longing for that parent. It is a child's right to experience their parents as equals, and to have their adult parents work in unity together for their well-being. However, the adverse nature of the litigation process can cause parents to lose sight of this truth.

Cases in which litigation is the focus of the divorce, whether the court determines a custody arrangement, or the parties ultimately settle custody matters relating to the children before trial, it is common for parties to carry the broken communication patterns, lack of trust, and competitive nature of the litigation process forward into post-divorce parenting. Many parents dig their heels in deeper and deeper, rather than searching for ways to better co-parent their children with a commitment to operate from a unified front — so their children feel truly anchored, safe, understood, loved, and cherished by both parents.

It is no wonder why children of litigated divorces find it hard to adjust and find their balance. The experiences they endure both during and after the litigation process can remain with them for decades and can provide an unfortunate model for their own interpersonal relationships. There is a high probability that these children will experience a divorce, or the dissolution of a partnership, in a manner similar to that of their parents.

It is my hope that this in-depth discussion of the litigation process provides you with a better understanding of what it really means to use the court system as the path to divorce. If you are already in the litigation process, no matter where you are in it, use the information you have learned, along with the tools in Part II, to assist you in achieving your best outcome.

# 9

# The Mediation Process

**M**ediation is a private, non-adversarial, interest-based process. Whereas litigation focuses on opposing *positions*, mediation focuses on the *interests* of each party when dealing with the subset issues. If divorcing parties desire a private process, are wanting to reach a settlement out of court, and are willing to negotiate in good faith, then mediation is a process that should be considered. A neutral facilitator trained in the mediation process will assist the parties in reaching their own resolution. There are mediation statutes in most jurisdictions that provide for the private and confidential nature of the process. Mediators must also adhere to certain ethical standards. All subset issues related to divorce can be resolved in mediation.

However, because mediation is a voluntary process, the issues that can be raised, and the possible resolutions reached, can be much broader than what is available through the litigation progress. A few examples include creative financial arrangements dealing with maintaining a jointly owned business or investment property, inspired parenting plans and child support arrangements, maintaining the former marital residence until a child graduates from high school, grandparents' or other extended family visitations, apportioning higher education costs (in those jurisdictions where courts do not), securing life insurance, maintaining health insurance for children beyond emancipation, as well as issues related to religious choices and/or training, vaccinations, and matters related to extracurricular activities that a court may not address.

Once the mediator determines that the case is suitable for mediation and the parties are comfortable proceeding, the parties engage in joint sessions with the mediator. Each party will have a chance to make introductory remarks that serve to inform the mediator and the other party of the issues important to them and what they desire to resolve in the mediation sessions. Just as important as setting forth the issues for discussion and resolution, the mediator provides a safe place in which the parties can share their feelings. As noted in the litigation section, there are times when a divorcing party simply wants to be heard. Providing the parties a platform to safely express and release their fears, to ask the hard "why" questions of each other, and to begin to release and shed feelings of guilt, betrayal, and unresolved resentments, will open the door to more meaningful discussions. The energy that attaches to unstated or unresolved emotions serves to block the creative spirit necessary for a successful mediation. This is not to say that the mediator is to be thought of as a replacement for therapy, coaching, or the counseling needs of the individual parties. However, when the parties can express their feelings without fear of judgment or ridicule from the other party, they are less likely to pursue a *position-based* posture and are more likely to communicate the underlying *interests* they have in a desired outcome.

To make it easier to understand the difference between a *position-based* desire and an *interest-based* desire, the following example uses a recreational vehicle as a marital asset to be distributed in the mediation process. Imagine that a husband, prior to the mediation session, holds the *position* that he should receive the parties' recreational vehicle because he was the party who introduced the camping lifestyle to the marriage. He firmly believes that this is the only resolution for this asset.

Now imagine that the wife, prior to the mediation session, holds the *position* that the recreational vehicle must be sold to a third party, and the proceeds from the sale must be used to pay off the parties' credit card debt. She firmly believes that maintaining the recreational vehicle would be irresponsible, and is closed to any other option.

Moreover, she believes that the reason her husband wants to keep the vehicle is to hurt her feelings. As noted above, when the parties are provided an opportunity to share thoughts that are important to each of them in the beginning of the mediation session, it creates an atmosphere that is more conducive to candid communication.

In this example, if the mediator were to ask the husband why it is important to him to keep the recreational vehicle, he will be more likely to communicate his underlying *interest*. As vulnerable as it may seem, when we explain the *interest* behind a particular desire, that not only softens the discussion and provides the other party with a deeper understanding, but also allows us to fully understand our own desire. A party may even change his mind once he begins to explain his reasoning.

Here, the husband explains that he intends to continue using the recreational vehicle for weekend camping trips with the parties' children. He adds that these outdoor excursions are special to him because it is the only time he can spend quality time with the children. The wife, upon hearing her husband's reasoning, may immediately recognize it as a deeper truth — that she had the children in her care while her husband was tending to work commitments. The weekend camping trips were a special time for the children; they love spending one-on-one time with their father and share his passion for the outdoors. The more a party understands the *interest* behind the other party's desired outcome, the more he or she is willing to consider meeting that *interest*.

In this example, it may be that the parties agree that the recreational vehicle should remain with the husband. The discussion may then move smoothly into placing a value on the vehicle, determining whether the wife will receive another marital asset as an offset, and how the credit card debt that concerned the wife will be otherwise addressed. Whenever a party understands the *interest* behind a request, he or she is more likely to consider the request from a neutral space, and not from the *position-based*, defensive posture of the traditional negotiation process.

In the litigation section, we discussed the use of the formal discovery process to gather information. The parties need information and documentation in order to make informed decisions. The information-gathering stage of the mediation process can be viewed as an informal discovery process. In fact, the mediation agreement between the parties and the mediator will typically include a provision that the parties agree to provide all pertinent information needed for each party to make informed choices. Together, the parties and the mediator will create a list of documents to be gathered, and any other information either party may have requested. In our recreational vehicle example, such documents might include statements showing the remaining loan balance on the vehicle, personal property tax statements related to the vehicle, vehicle industry guides to assist in the valuation, as well as monthly credit card statements showing the liability about which the wife is concerned.

Once the appropriate information has been gathered and reviewed, the mediator facilitates the parties in the process of discussing the issues to be resolved, the brainstorming of potential options, the evaluation of the options proposed, and, finally, reaching a final resolution of the issues raised. It is important to note that the brainstorming session is critically important to a tailored resolution. Each party must be free to throw out options, regardless of how extreme, silly, or unlikely they might seem. Just like the process of a think tank, the parties must be able to share all ideas and options that come to them in a free-flowing stream of consciousness, without judgment or evaluation from themselves, their spouse or the mediator facilitating the session. Of course, many of these concepts and proposed options will be dismissed once the evaluation stage begins; however, it is this free flow of creative ideas that becomes the material from which personalized marital agreements are reached. Therefore, the environment, respectful communication guidelines, and the concept of *interests* as opposed to *positions* must be honored if the mediation is to be successful.

A mediator cannot provide legal advice to either party. However, if the mediator is also an attorney, in most jurisdictions, in addition to providing "legal information" to the clients, he or she can provide a more "evaluative" mediation and point out the strengths and weaknesses of an option proposed. He or she can also suggest likely outcomes, if an issue were to be decided by the court. There may be times in the process when a party may be uncomfortable sharing certain information, or may have trouble understanding what is being shared. Since private caucuses with the mediator are available for this purpose, the mediator may request a private caucus if he or she feels it would be helpful. This safeguard is in place so that the mediation does not fail due to a party's discomfort, a misunderstanding, or a lack of knowledge. Many times, a quick private caucus with the mediator will serve to bring a challenging session back into focus.

The mediation process is flexible and can be extremely accommodating. If additional information or specialized assistance is required by the parties to reach certain decisions, neutral professionals can be retained by the parties to assist in the mediation process. As an example, parties may agree in a mediation session that the fair market value of their real property will be determined by a certified real estate appraiser before they schedule their next mediation session. Additionally, parties might agree to retain a neutral child specialist to assist them with issues concerning the custody of their children, and to create an individualized parenting plan. A financial advisor may be retained to assist in the financial aspects of the mediated settlement.

Mediation is a good option for parties who choose to avoid the harshness of the court system. Nothing expressed, disclosed, or otherwise shared in the mediation process can be used by either party if the meditation fails, a point that is invaluable when dealing with sensitive issues. It is important to note, however, that mediators are mandatory reporters in most states; if a mediator suspects that a child is being abused or neglected, he or she must report the abuse to the proper authorities. Be mindful as well that any information and/or documentation that can be obtained through the formal litigation discovery process does *not* remain confidential, should the case proceed to litigation.

It is recommended that you have a consultation with, and consider retaining, an attorney prior to starting the mediation process. This recommendation applies even if the mediator selected is also an attorney. Once an attorney is retained, you will have access to him or her throughout the mediation process to provide separate legal advice, to answer any questions, and to review your mediated settlement agreement prior to signing. If you have chosen mediation as your preferred divorce process, inform the attorney during your initial consultation. If you would like to engage in the mediation process but feel uncomfortable sitting in a conference room with your spouse and the mediator, you can make a request for your attorney (or both attorneys, if your spouse has also retained counsel) to attend the mediation sessions.

However, please note that the intimacy and the tone of the mediation sessions will change when attorneys are physically present — as opposed to simply having them available for consultation outside of the sessions. Moreover, the depth of the communication shared is always altered when additional parties are present.

Since a mediated agreement will affect your legal rights, it is to be treated as an enforceable contract. Therefore, it is imperative to fully understand what you are agreeing to, especially if your document contains personally crafted resolutions on certain issues that would be considered outside general laws or guidelines. Parties who take the time to plan, to understand, and to be creative in their approach to reaching a resolution, are more likely to have long-term success and rest more comfortably with, and honor, the agreements they reach in mediation.

It should be noted that mediation used at the beginning of the divorce process has important differences to mediation sessions used while engaged in litigation. Mediation that is sought to avoid a looming trial, after a long, arduous litigation process, is fraught with the same fear and animosity fostered throughout the litigation. Rather than negotiating from an *interest-based* perspective, the parties have been conditioned in litigation to perpetuate their *position-based* mindsets. Mediated agreements that are reached under these conditions, no matter how talented the mediator, are nothing more than an attempt to stop the litigation. They rarely, if ever, result in solid, long-term resolutions. However, mediation is still preferred over going to trial as it allows you to maintain some control over the outcome.

In addition to the potential of reaching an agreement both parties are comfortable with — a "win-win" result, to the extent possible — the mediation process is financially friendly to the family. The cost of the mediation is limited to the hourly rate of the mediator, the number of sessions required to reach an agreement, and the fees paid to third-party professionals and attorneys who provide guidance and advice throughout the process. The cost will naturally increase if the attorneys are asked to attend the mediation sessions. Accordingly, the savings in terms of the financial and emotional cost to the family is significantly reduced from the cost of litigation.

## *An Unexpected Turn of Grace*

I was in the middle of the second mediation session with a couple who had two young children when I felt there was no hope that the mediation would be successful. Despite a somewhat cordial first session, the opening statement made by each party was short and to the point. One said, "I just want to resolve what we need to resolve," and the other responded, "I agree." It did not matter how much I pushed them for details; there was nothing more either wanted to say. From my initial telephone discussion with each party prior to the mediation session, I knew there had been infidelity, and a misuse of marital funds at the heart of the dissolution of the marriage. It was mutually decided that the first session would wrap up early. Each party was given a list of information and documentation that was to be gathered and brought to the next mediation session.

The parties arrived separately to the second session, with the documentation and information requested in hand. But not long after the doors to my conference room closed, a warzone ensued. Each word, each glance outside the window, even a peek at a cellphone by either party, would elicit an immediate emotional reaction from the other party.

It is certainly normal for parties in mediation to be emotional; however, the pattern of communication established by this couple was not conducive to mediation at all. Despite a separate caucus with each party, and the written mediation agreement the parties had read and signed, setting forth rules of conduct, I was unable to gain control of the session enough to stop their yelling, accusations, and extreme bitterness. Each issue was summarily pushed to a symbolic "parking lot" to be addressed later. The couple was unable to resolve even one minor issue so they could use that momentum to move on. Each issue became a screaming match, curse words were volleyed back and forth, and there was a complete unwillingness to show any respect for the process, me, and more importantly, each other. There was absolutely no willingness to retain the services of a third party to assist with their communication. It was black-and-white; either I helped them resolve their case, or they would continue straight to litigation.

I knew that if I terminated the mediation session, the couple's entire savings would be exhausted litigating. Their two adorable children, whose pictures were on the table at my request, would be exposed to even more trauma. The family would forever be entangled in the web of litigation. For me, this would be the first failed mediation in my career.

While they continued arguing, I sat in silence and played out their probable futures in my mind. I knew that there are only two emotions, love, and fear. Everything these parties were experiencing: the rage, the resentment, the blame, the jealousy, the hate, the shame, the hurt, and the betrayal, were all coming from a place of fear.

With limited time and no possibility of working with them using the tools discussed in Part II of this book, I thought if I could just somehow get them into the energy of love, even for a brief moment, they might have a breakthrough.

I stood up to get their attention, announcing that I would be leaving the room for five minutes. With a calm voice, I instructed them to silently consider one thing that they admired about the other person during that time. Then, I asked that they share this sentiment with the other person before my return.

As soon as I left, I heard their voices raised in anger once again. In my office, I stood in front of a bookshelf that rested against the wall adjacent to the conference room. I slipped into a meditative state and requested that I be filled with unconditional love. Within a few seconds, I began to feel my heart expand. Energetically, I sent this love through the wall and into the conference room for several minutes.

Once I returned to the conference room, I could not believe what I saw through the glass-paneled conference room doors: My clients were standing in front of the window, in a loving embrace! I almost cried, and waited a few seconds before entering the room.

The couple took their seats, apologizing to me and to each other for their previous behavior. They briefly described what they admired about the other person. Both came to the realization that, despite everything, they loved each other very deeply. However, they were just not suited to live together as husband and wife. Although finding it difficult to explain considering the rollercoaster ride their relationship had been on for the past two years, they were both determined to work with me to reach a settlement that would benefit their family.

Within the two remaining sessions, the couple successfully reached an amicable resolution of all issues — including not only an acceptable division of assets, but also a shared parenting plan. The parties also agreed to meet with a child specialist before I completed the mediated settlement agreement for their attorneys' review; that way, they would have another parenting resource in the event an issue related to the parenting plan arose.

One year later, they engaged me again, to mediate a modification to the child support arrangement. They relayed how pleased they were with their co-parenting experience. They were both now in new relationships and even joined their new significant others, and their children, for barbeques, birthday celebrations, and other family events.

Over the years, this couple has referred several new clients to me. By being able to forgive each other so completely and move forward with only the *jewels* of their relationship, as opposed to their initial bitterness and recrimination, the lives of the now-divorced couple and their children will be forever blessed.

Whatever divine energy graced this couple and redirected their paths, I will be forever grateful to have been a part of their success.

# 10

# The Collaborative Process

Similar to the mediation process, the collaborative process has been referred to as a "peaceful divorce," a "no-court divorce," or, as this author prefers to call it, "a divorce with dignity." Unlike the mediation process, whereby the attorneys are involved tangentially outside of the mediation sessions (if at all), the collaborative process involves the parties and their attorneys from the beginning.

The parties sign a collaborative participation agreement whereby they commit to making a good-faith effort in their negotiation of a mutually agreed upon, interest-based resolution — without litigation. The collaborative participation agreement also provides that each party will voluntarily disclose all relevant information needed to foster informed discussions and decision-making. The parties must each be represented by an attorney who has been trained in the collaborative process, whose representation will terminate should either party initiate a contested court proceeding.

The collaborative process also includes an extended team approach, whereby other neutral, collaboratively trained professionals may be engaged to assist in the process. A financial professional may be engaged to assist with the financial restructuring of the marital estate; a neutral mental health professional may be engaged to support the emotional and communication needs of the parties; a child specialist may be engaged to assist in developing a sound parenting plan. In most collaborative agreements, the engagement of these professionals will also terminate if either party initiates a contested court proceeding.

The collaborative training of all professionals is essential. It requires commitment, training, and the ability to see all facets of an issue in order to successfully navigate through the process. The professionals must share the intention to provide a collection of all knowledge, skill and wisdom in a shared environment so that the divorcing parties may achieve a comprehensive agreement that meets the interests of both parties, and will be honored and durable. There is no room for ego on the part of the professionals; therefore, any need to be "right" must be tamed and monitored. The collaborative process is more akin to a think tank than to a boxing ring or courtroom.

In a traditional litigation process, the attorney is hired and charged with zealously representing only their client's position, regardless of any consequences to the opposing party. There are times when an attorney is not in agreement, or on board, with their client's position on a matter; however, they must continue to advocate that position in litigation to the best of their ability. Distasteful client beliefs and behaviors that may call into question basic differences between client and attorney are usually experienced in silence.

In a collaborative environment, the attorneys are asked to share legal knowledge and wisdom, and not to withhold information. They are asked to participate in the discovery and creation of mutual solutions so that the *interests* of both parties may be addressed and satisfied. A successful collaborative process requires an atmosphere of compassion, dignity and respect for both parties.

Similarly, decisions concerning the well-being of the children of the marriage are considered paramount to any self-serving desire held by a party as it relates to custodial matters. Legal information and advice are expected to be provided in joint collaborative sessions to prevent the common: "my attorney said this" argument so prevalent in traditional litigation cases. This is not to suggest that a party may not communicate privately with his or her attorney in the collaborative process; it simply means that when information is shared in an open environment, the need for, or the desire to, privately "strategize" suddenly loses its luster. The collaborative strategy becomes an outward blending of ideas and possibilities for the whole, or "we," rather than an inward or "me" focused process.

The cost of the collaborative process is not inexpensive; however, most attorneys agree that the cost of the collaborative process is typically one-third the cost of traditional litigation. The voluntary disclosure of information is significantly less costly than formal discovery in the litigation process. The parties may choose to complete the collaborative case with just their respective attorneys and no other professionals. If expert input is desired for a particular issue, one neutral, collaboratively trained professional (such as a child specialist) may be added to the team, as opposed to the hiring of two opposing experts in litigation.

In terms of the emotional cost, there is no perfect process that magically dissolves the emotions associated with a major life transition. However, unlike the litigation process, where heightened emotions and sometimes downright abusive behavior is the norm, the collaborative process attempts to soften these emotions through compassion. The collaborative process provides safety rather than uncertainty. The exposure of personal information is accomplished with respect and dignity. The team shares pertinent information and engages in *interest-based* discussions with a unity consciousness. Most importantly, the team promotes the visioning of a promising future for all involved, rather than a recitation and anchoring of past experiences, the vanguard attributes of the traditional litigation process.

## *The Shepherd of Truth*

I wanted to share one collaborative case that inspired me greatly. The parties had been married for over ten years; I represented the wife. Our team also included a neutral financial advisor to assist in the prudent division of a complicated marital estate. In four separate collaborative sessions, the team was able to assist the parties in reaching a comprehensive settlement agreement. Real property was assessed, a small family business was evaluated, and the multi-layered division of the marital estate was crafted in a manner far removed from what a court has the power to accomplish. The party's communication throughout the process was as good as we could have expected under the circumstances. Most of the communication in the collaborative sessions was forward-looking. Any backward look into the details of the marriage was limited to the information necessary to craft an agreement.

Once the agreement was drafted and agreed upon by the parties, the collaborative team met in my office for the formal signing. Suddenly, seemingly out of character and out of the blue, my client forcefully announced that she would not sign the agreement, and, moreover, that she wanted custody of the parties' dog, a German Shepherd.

My client's demand surprised and angered her husband, because he believed that all issues had been resolved. He shouted that his wife hated the dog and that she spent years complaining about the dirt the dog tracked into the house, the dog hair left on all surfaces, and waking up to the dog sleeping in their bed; also, she could not stand the dog's odor, despite her husband's efforts to bathe the dog weekly. There was never doubt that the husband would retain ownership of the German Shepherd.

As her attorney, I too was surprised at this last-minute change of heart, as it was clear in the negotiations that the parties' dog would remain in the husband's care. Because this was a collaborative case, rather than initiating a private discussion with my client I asked her right there in the conference room, to share with the team what was in her heart regarding her interest in the German Shepherd. With tears in her eyes, she began to explain that, after years of unsuccessfully trying to conceive a baby, including months of expensive fertility treatments, she realized that this dog had become her child. Despite her annoyance with having to continually clean after him, she realized she was actually parenting the dog. Surprisingly, she discovered this activity brought her joy and comfort, and filled the empty space in her heart that was waiting for the child she desired.

The safety of the collaborative environment, together with my prompting, allowed her to speak honestly from her heart. My client was able to share her interest in the German Shepherd with the team, and trust that we would hear her feelings without further criticism. The husband was moved by this development, and tried hard to hold back his own tears, admitting that he had no idea of her true feelings about the dog.

Accordingly, after the husband offered to share custody of the German Shepherd, the team drafted an official "parenting schedule" for inclusion in the parties' agreement, which was signed at the end of the meeting. My client left, excited that it was her weekend to spend "parenting time" with her "baby." The love of this dog served to "shepherd in" the truth within my client's heart and allowed her to enjoy the wonderful gifts this animal's life would bring into hers.

# 11

# Self-Negotiated – Hybrid Process

When parties can communicate well despite their impending divorce, they can choose to resolve the issues related to their divorce, both together and privately. This approach has been referred to as the "kitchen-table" process. However, this name can be misleading. Engaging in kitchen-table discussions to keep down the cost of the divorce process does not mean the participants should not be informed about potential decisions. Absolutely make the effort to become familiar with your legal rights through a consultation with a local attorney. It is also important to engage in an informal discovery process, so you have the necessary information to properly address each issue. Your attorney will assist you in creating a structure for your discussions, and will give you a list of documentation and other information you may need.

As a brief example, we will look at one factor in a discussion concerning spousal support. It may be pointless for a party to engage in spousal support discussions with his or her spouse without a thorough understanding of what constitutes "income" for spousal support purposes. Hence, you need to know how "income" is defined in your jurisdiction and how to have a structured approach to the discussion.

In this example, let us assume that one party earns no income, and the other party earns a yearly salary of $150,000. Without speaking to legal counsel, the parties agree that they will use the net income as shown on the employed spouse's paystub, as opposed to the gross income, when determining a monthly support amount for the non-earning spouse. Now let us assume that each month the earning spouse makes mandatory contributions to a 401(k) retirement account that is deducted from his or her gross pay. In addition to these mandatory contributions, the earning spouse makes an additional $1,200 contribution to his or her 401(k) retirement account each month; this is also deducted from his or her gross pay.

The non-earning spouse might easily miss the fact that, if the earning spouse were not making these extra, voluntary contributions to his or her retirement account, there would be an additional $14,400 annually in "income," as the parties have agreed to define it, that would be available to satisfy the spousal support obligation. If the receiving spouse signs a binding, written agreement setting forth a monthly spousal support amount that is less than what he or she *could* have received had the additional income been included in the calculation, he or she may have no recourse to change it.

In most jurisdictions, the agreement in this example would not be modifiable, absent a finding that would render the contract void, such as a finding of fraud, duress, unconscionability, or undue influence. Otherwise, the spousal support, as provided in the signed agreement of the parties, would be binding and enforceable, unless and until there is a compelling change of circumstances and a court-ordered modification.

Unfortunately, buyer's remorse does not apply to marital settlement agreements. Moreover, if one party has legal counsel and the other party operates without legal counsel, this will have no effect on the validity of a marital settlement agreement. Thus, it is important to be prudent in your private negotiations, and fully informed. Moreover, it is extremely important to have your attorney review any written agreement prior to your signing it.

A hybrid approach that includes private negotiations on the subset issues of the divorce can be a savvy, holistic and graceful approach to reaching a marital settlement agreement. However, it is best suited for parties who have been fully informed of the law in their jurisdiction, and who have also engaged in a process of thorough informal discovery, so they have everything they need to make informed decisions. If private discussions become difficult, a hybrid approach might include participating in a four-way settlement conference, with the parties' attorneys present.

If the attorneys understand that it is the desire of both parties to reach a settlement outside of court, and that the process be cost-effective, they can assist the parties in preparing for the settlement conference, be present to guide the discussion, provide real-time legal advice to their respective clients, draft a comprehensive marital settlement agreement once a resolution is reached, and facilitate the divorce itself.

## The Long Road Home

I represented a woman who had one child from her marriage. Her daughter had just started middle school when my client decided she could no longer stay in the marriage.

She and her husband owned a residence a few blocks from their daughter's school. During our initial consultation, this client was adamant that she wanted to keep the family residence, and that her husband "owed her that much!" Arguments with her husband had become a daily occurrence, and the animosity within the house had become unbearable. The parties' daughter was embarrassed to be in public with her parents, and stopped inviting her friends to the residence, fearing her parents' behavior.

By the end of our consultation, this client decided she would like the opportunity to work things out with her husband directly. She wanted to use attorneys, if possible, for guidance rather than having them facilitate communication. We scheduled another consultation, during which we discussed the law for each issue in more detail, as well as potential resolutions that would be outside the court's jurisdiction to order, but might be more suited for their family.

I provided her with a structure for communicating with her husband, and a list of additional documentation and information she would need prior to initiating these discussions. Over the next few weeks, and between her discussions with her husband, I received emails and telephone calls from my client, requesting clarification on certain matters and discussing the probable resolutions she and her husband were considering. Surprisingly, by the end of the third week, this client scheduled an appointment for the purpose of discussing the agreements she had reached on all sub-issues with her husband, and requested I memorialize these agreements in a formal document.

Knowing the family residence was important to her, I was surprised when she described the final resolution of this asset.

It was a creative variation of an option I suggested, and was certainly outside the boundaries of what a court could grant on its own. My client traveled an hour each way for work. Her husband, on the other hand, worked very close to the family residence, and enjoyed a flexible schedule. Her husband was the parent who provided school and other transportation for their daughter and was home two to three hours earlier than my client on most days. It was during these discussions that each party expressed the desire for their daughter to remain in the same school and residence, if possible.

Ultimately, the parties decided that my client would move out of the marital residence and into a rented condominium, with amenities such as a swimming pool, tennis court and recreation room that their daughter would enjoy when she was in my client's care. The husband would remain in the family residence, either until such time as their daughter graduated from high school, or until the husband chose to relocate. When the property was sold, the parents would equally share the net proceeds. The husband would be responsible for all expenses related to the property, and my client would be responsible for her lease payments. If the husband chose to relocate from the residence prior to their daughter's graduation, my client would then have the opportunity to buy-out her husband's interest.

The parties' daughter accompanied my client during the search for the perfect condominium and was over the moon with excitement that she would have access to a swimming pool and tennis court right on the property, as well as a recreation room to host get-togethers with her friends. Although my client agreed to less parenting time, she recognized that she was not as available as her husband to meet her daughter's daily needs, and that the arrangement was really in her daughter's best interests. All remaining issues flowed easily once they reached an agreement on custody and living arrangements. At the end of their one-year separation period, I facilitated the divorce with her husband's attorney.

Both clients reported that the arrangement was working well for them, and were so thankful that both attorneys promoted the idea that they were in the best position to craft a settlement agreement that would meet the needs of their family. The family transitioned into one that actually works for them. Waiting until their daughter graduates high school may seem like a long way home to a final resolution on this asset; however, it is a journey each party was happy to travel.

Whether you choose litigation, mediation, collaborative, or a self-negotiated/hybrid process, be sure that it is one that will work for you and your family. There is no one-size-fits-all approach. I do recommend, if possible, that you avoid litigation as a first step, and focus your emotional and financial resources to secure the assistance you "need," rather than becoming entangled in a process that takes control of your journey. The different divorce options available, and which would be the right fit for your family, is a discussion that you should have with your spouse in the early stages of the divorce process. This communication will dictate the type of attorney you will be looking for, will provide an indication of how you both might communicate in a mediation or a self-directed option, and will start the process of learning to work together, rather than against each other.

The parties who achieve the best results reach this level of conscious communication and decision-making early in the divorce. The system has a way of feeding on the energy of people in turmoil — that is, unless the divorcing parties become active participants in setting the stage, so the players involved work for them in a manner that is in the best interests of their family. It is understood that not all divorces can be handled holistically; however, most divorcing couples, when aware of their options beforehand, would rather experience a process tailored to their unique situation, as opposed to traditional litigation.

# PART II

# The Soul's Journey

Whether you are contemplating divorce, currently engaged in the divorce process, or have previously been touched by the tentacles of divorce, recognizing this event as a pivotal step in your soul's journey is essential. All transitions bring with them the opportunity to uncover the jewels of the experience. These jewels reveal themselves in many forms; however, they shine the brightest when they take the form of the wisdom that serves as a catalyst for our soul's evolution. Within the transition of divorce is a treasure chest of jewels waiting to be discovered. I invite you to join me in the excavation process.

# 12

# The Magic of Discovering Who We Really Are

When we open the door to the fullness of who we really are, we begin to view our life as more than the bones, flesh, and blood of the physical body that carries us through our human experience. We begin to acknowledge that eternal part of us — our essence, our light, our spirit, the pure Divine Source, the Creative Source, God, the Divine Universe, the Greater Intelligence, the Great Spirit (whatever label is best suited for you) — that is present in all living things and has no beginning and no end.

Throughout the rest of this book, I have chosen "the Divine Source" to communicate this understanding. Its mystical light glows dimly within our heart and becomes stronger and brighter as our awareness expands. We discover this essential part of ourselves when we are ready to ask the questions that every individual asks at some point on their journey: "Who am I?" "Why am I here?" "What is my purpose?" It is at this moment when our journey becomes a "soul journey," and not simply a human experience. When we make the conscious choice to greet this essential part of ourselves with a gentle hand filled with curiosity and reverence, we begin to discover our greater truth.

Most of us have grown accustomed to being told that we are small, that we are not good enough, and that we are unworthy. We have been flooded with both suggestions and demands of how we are to live our lives, and what is expected of us. We have been indoctrinated into being good boys and girls, to assimilate into what others have defined as "normal" and "proper." As a result, we have buried our inner urges and spent our lives looking for answers, approval, and acceptance outside of ourselves. We bury our inner urges to break out of the box of what we know as our life, and label these urges as bad, dirty, scandalous, ungrateful, and at times, sinful. Whether the programs that run our lives are rooted in family and ancestral traditions, communities, culture, past lives, the legal system, the educational system, religious organizations, the media, or other hierarchical structures, our perception of the world, and of ourselves, has been shaped by these outside influences. Our personal experiences within this artificial framework contribute to how we perceive the world, and how we view ourselves and others, and have a great influence on how we respond to life and make the choices that affect our lives.

Every decision we make or situation we encounter is highly influenced by this backdrop. Accordingly, our belief system, which is rooted in a combination of outside influences, and our own experiences within this structured casing are limiting. These limiting beliefs — and our attachment to them — is the source of our suffering. As we humbly surrender one limiting belief after another to be examined in the light of our true essence, we begin the journey of awakening.

There, we learn that it is our own pure essence, our light, our spirit, which illuminates and powers the soul. The soul can be understood as the vehicle that holds our blueprint, our divine architect's plan. It is this part of us that journeys on with our spirit, once we are freed from the human vessel that facilitates our earthbound experience. The soul holds our personality, our cognizance, our emotions, the lessons, gifts, and knowledge we have gained during this lifetime — as well as all the other lifetimes we have experienced on earth and in the multiverse, among all the different dimensions.

This collection of information has been referred to by many as our sacred book, our book of life, or our Akashic Records. There are many who believe that the Akashic Records are limited to our earthly experiences. It is my belief, however, that when we step outside of our earthly paradigm of linear time, we understand that all experiences are happening at once, in what is described as the "now" — and that we are experiencing, and have access to, every experience or "now moment," whenever or wherever the experience may be happening.

The elixir to the challenges of our human journey begins with the understanding that we are each a soul, a pure being of light, having a human experience, on purpose, and with a mission. Everything that happens while we are wearing our human costume is part of a divinely orchestrated play we helped birth. The difference between a human-designed play and the play that has been crafted by the soul can be summed up in the word *probabilities*. Both versions include a major plot as well as sub-plots, main characters, supporting characters, extras, and an overall theme.

However, unlike a human-designed play, the soul's play is devoid of the predetermined written script. Other than a handful of details and a few major agreements with other soul travelers, the acts associated with the soul's play are manifested through probabilities. There are a multitude of ways in which our soul can experience what it intends during a lifetime. We are living on a planet of free choice; it is therefore our choice which path or paths we choose to explore once we have started our sojourn on earth. The characters on the journey with us have their own soul's plan, as well as the same freedom of choice. The synchronicities of many elements must occur for the acts that make up our uniquely crafted play to manifest into reality. We have all felt the irony associated with the "best laid plans." The good news is, there are no wrong choices. In fact, for every choice we make, there is a part of our soul that plays out the alternative.

Deep within us lives a wise sage. The soul is the vessel of truth, and the source of all wisdom. While wearing our human shoes and using our ego-mind as our guide, we blindly walk on the floor of the valley. Our higher self, the part of us that remains beyond the veil in the spirit world, is perched high on the mountain-top and, with an expanded view, can see both sides of the mountain's terrain. Unaware that we too can have a bird's-eye view, we plunge ahead, dragging our stories, our pains, our woundedness, our limiting belief systems, and our dense physical bodies — until the moment we are met with a messenger of hope.

This messenger may be in the form of an event that shakes us to our core, and so awakens us from our dream state. It may appear following the passing of a loved one — or the separation from any anchor we have put in place — leaving us feeling abandoned, scared, and unable to find our balance. This messenger may come in the form of a human messenger who just happens to say the right thing, at the right time, in the right way; we know within the depths of our being that there is truth in the message being shared. Whatever it is that causes us to choose to pause the turning of the wheel of our life long enough to explore the answer to the question of who we really are, and so directs us to the path of our own enlightenment, is a true blessing of grace. If divorce happens to be your messenger, embrace it, and explore the messages and *jewels* that are meant for you to find as you proceed forward.

As we stand in our human shoes, we perceive our current life experiences, as well as our past lifetimes, to be in a linear progression; for the soul, however, every lifetime is viewed as happening all at once. Put simply, there is no past, present or future orientation; time is an illusion. As quantum physics has shown us, time past, time present, and time future are simultaneously occurring. The modern science of String Theory has shown that the universe operates with ten dimensions; and many people believe that there are an infinite number of dimensions. It is said that beyond our Milky Way galaxy are upwards of two trillion additional galaxies within our observable universe. Thus, if the universe is defined as only what we can observe, how many additional universes might exist beyond our observational capability?

The concept that we are alone in the universe or the multiverse — that we are the only life force — is fast becoming a myth among more and more people. As we expand our inner awareness, we begin to connect with the vastness of our true essence and the expansiveness of our true existence.

We are each unique sparks of the Divine Source, which naturally means that the Divine Source resides within each of us. If we are made in the image of the Divine Source, then we are each naturally divine and can never be separated; we are tethered to each other and to our source. The Divine Source is pure loving energy, energy is eternal — therefore, we are eternal, infinite beings. It is through the manipulation of this divine energy that the intelligent framework of the universe, which includes us, has been created. Energy is constantly in motion. Science has demonstrated that everything in the universe is made from the same energy source and that all things, seen and unseen, are vibrating at differing frequencies. Thus, everything that occurs in the universe is caused by some manipulation of the fluctuating frequencies.

The cells of our bodies communicate by means of a network of resonance or coherence frequency. The cells of plant life communicate by this same resonance. The reality we each perceive has been created by our thoughts, emotions and actions working to manipulate this intelligent energy. We must remember that our thoughts, emotions, and all actions that follow have been influenced within the constructs of our own inner belief system. Unlike plants, which are devoid of these predispositions until they are introduced to influences outside their own true essence, as humans we are influenced from the moment our souls enter our mothers' wombs. On a grander scale, the reality of the human collective as we experience it, has been created by the predominant thoughts, emotions and actions of the majority of the collective. When we recognize and disavow these external influences, we begin the journey of remembering the power of the Divine Source, which resides within each of us, and thus we begin to reclaim our own sovereignty.

The Divine Source is expressing itself through us in a multitude of experiences, here on earth as well as in other dimensional timelines. As humans, we have been gifted with an evolved consciousness. We are created from the highest vibrational frequency, that of love. Love is a label that humans have given to a sacred, unexplainable, benevolent, omnipresent, and omnificent emotion — the same emotion and reverence we experience when connecting with the Divine Source. Love is the frequency of the many names we have attached to the Divine Source to aid in our understanding.

It is our human need for identification that causes some people to give this source a human image, with a personality that corresponds to that of our human ego. Rather than blending with the Divine Source — with the knowing that we are in constant co-creation together, that the Divine Source is within us, that we are made from the Divine Source, and are therefore, the Divine Source itself — we view ourselves as separate. This belief in our separateness creates a void in our heart that we search throughout our entire lives to fill. However, the eternal flame of our true essence burns gently within our hearts, waiting for us to notice, and remember its presence. This is more powerful evidence of the intelligent source of which we are part.

As we stretch our understanding further, the concept that we have experienced life on other planets within our galaxy and perhaps beyond, and that we are intimately connected to other beings living outside of our perceptional reality, is gaining momentum. As we gaze in the direction of the stars, is it possible that we have a much larger family in other parts of the universe? Is it possible that our larger galactic family is aware of our presence? Is it possible that our joint mission on earth is much broader than our own personal development and evolution, individually and collectively? Is it possible that within our own DNA lives the power that supersedes our human-created technologies?

Is it possible that we are living in one or more dimensional realities that far exceed the consciousness of our current understanding? Is it possible that our consciousness has been interfered with by other beings of light? Is it possible that we are a hybrid race? Is it possible that the duality that makes up the fabric of our existence is intentional? Is it possible that the wars we experience on earth are replications of a much larger galactic war taking place in a dimensional space beyond our awareness? Could the light-versus-dark paradigms be part of a much broader understanding than our collective scriptures and philosophers have indicated? Is it possible that we were involved in the seeding of this planet, and perhaps have engaged in this process many times before? Is it possible that the "creation story" is much broader than we have been led to believe?

And, finally, is it possible that we are all on a journey of remembering who we really are, while simultaneously raising our consciousness to the place of our own sovereign divinity?

Wherever our personal beliefs may rest within these potentials, we are all beginning to rip open the box of possibilities on our search to discover our truth and to find our way back home. Whatever road we choose to walk on this journey, if we allow our soul and higher self to guide us, we will have a much smoother and safer experience. As souls, we are all headed in the same direction, and are destined to return home safely. We will not fully comprehend the larger concept of "home" until we have returned to the spirit world.

However, we know that the Divine Source is an energy of pure love and, as such, is the greatest tool we have for making the best of our human experience, and is also the key to our soul's evolution. Love is an alchemical force that can transform fear. Love is our truth and is eternal. Those emotions that come from the energy of love include compassion, empathy, forgiveness, and freedom. If love is of the light, then fear is anything outside of the light, and is illusory. The flame within us is fueled with the gift of free will. Flames can burn, flames can enlighten, and flames can also destroy. We must use our flame to shine a light on our shadow, and use our love to transform all the lower frequencies we have been branded with. As we each ascend by the power of our own natural essence, we provide the momentum, courage, and space for others to bear witness to our transformation, and to know that they too have this powerful force within them to do the same.

Divorce is life changing. It is a life transition with the ability to catapult our awakening, to reunite us with our true essence, to encourage us to take back our power, and it provides the opportunity for us to pivot our life in the direction of our soul's intended path. We are here to evolve. Divorce is a symbolic knock on the door of our inner being, prompting us to pay a visit. It is an important pause in our life, and is ripe with opportunities. Divorce is also a human experience that triggers all our insecurities and fears. It is a time when every emotion available in this human experience is running through us at full speed. It is hard to go within when our external environment is in a state of confusion and chaos, and life as we knew it is spinning with uncertainty.

However, we must recognize that how we respond to the stimulus is a direct result of the paradigms that have followed us since birth, and perhaps have even been carried over from other lifetimes.

Once we become familiar with the legal process, as you are doing with your research and by reading Part I of this book, space will open for you to go beyond the physical noise of the divorce, so you can begin a simultaneous healing journey that will allow you to come forward from your soul.

If you are experiencing any feelings of distress as it relates to time or the timing of your divorce, I ask that you allow yourself to step out of your time-conscious predisposition for the remainder of this book, since the concept of time can operate like a chokehold on your psyche. However, once we release the patterns we have developed as they relate to our perception of time, our psyche experiences its natural state of freedom and discovers limitless possibilities.

As we examine our lives, we begin to see the gift in recognizing our life as a platform of truth, our truth. All the twists and turns we experience, even those that take us off-course, are those our souls set out to experience and to learn from — devouring the richness from each encounter, from each moment of laughter, from each tear that is shed, from each raw emotion that surfaces from happy, sad, and even tragic experiences — to taste the spices from the variety of contrasting circumstances as we travel the road to enlightenment. Even when we cannot see through the illusion of separateness and we swim in the depths that lead us to despair, a time that has been termed "the dark night of the soul," we will find ourselves at the surface once again, greeted by the light of the sun.

It is through all experiences, even when they are simply basking in the spirit of being, that we are growing, learning, expanding, and becoming beacons of light that will guide us forward, as well as shine brightly for others. Just as a lighthouse beams a comforting light indicating that the shore is nearby, we too are meant to serve and to be the light for others during a time when their inner compass may have lost its calibration. During a divorce, our inner compass is naturally in a state of misalignment. The focus must be on the light of our own truth, even while we seek external support. As we alchemize and transform our old belief systems and patterns into our new signature of truth, we must also respect the process and the truth of all others. This is challenging for us to accomplish when moving through a divorce; however, the more inner work we do, the more we understand its benefits.

If we are each unique expressions of the Divine Source, it means there is no other being who shares our combination of characteristics, our gifts. Accordingly, we are the only ones who can share the gifts our souls intended to express and share with others. It is this uniqueness that makes us beautiful, and it is this same uniqueness that causes us to battle when we hold the belief that our truth is the only truth. Truth is simply a matter of frequency, and, just like a radio receiver, there are many stations for us to choose from. When we align with the frequency of our divine nature, we can ride the fluctuating waves of our experiences, knowing we are safe within the raft of our own inner faith — knowing that all is well with our soul, regardless of how we may be perceiving our reality. At times, we may feel lost and as small as a droplet of water within a vast ocean; however, we must never forget that *we are also the ocean.*

Wherever you are on your journey, I honor you and all your experiences. As we explore more of the fullness of who we are, and how divorce can be a catalyst for an amazing understanding of ourselves and those around us, I ask that you take in what you need from these pages and leave behind what may not resonate with you. If I can shed light on just one important facet of your journey, my heart will be full, and I will rejoice in knowing that I answered the call of my soul to fulfill this important mission by writing this book.

# 13

# The Soul's Plan and Team in Spirit

### *Preincarnation Plan*

**P**rior to this incarnation, as a soul being, we each planned with other members of our soul family, our guides and our higher master teachers what we wanted to explore, experience, contribute, and learn in this lifetime. We also plan and coordinate with our soul group the roles we will perform for each other throughout our lifetimes — parents, siblings, extended family members, children, friends, spouses and significant others, colleagues, and the many souls who will perform brief cameos. In the spirit world, we work with our larger soul family, as well as with other certain soul groups depending on our development and needs. We travel with our soul family through many incarnations, playing differing roles for each other, all of which will assist in our soul's evolution.

We each choose the parents to whom we will be born, the country, the culture, the ancestral line, belief systems, and most importantly, the intimate circumstances associated with our chosen family. If we step back and consider those individuals who make up our human family, we will notice certain themes playing out within the larger group. Similarly, when we look, we can see certain themes that exist within our relationships with friends, colleagues, and other individuals with whom we have a close relationship. A focus on the core of these relationships will reveal their higher purpose. Unlike a stage play with its tightly arranged script, timing and scheduled acts that leave no room for error and improvisation, our life plan, or "play," can be viewed in terms of potentials and probabilities. Certain events are pre-planned or "pre-destined," but the timing, potency and legitimacy of these events are subject to our free will, as well as the free will of the souls journeying with us. Once we incarnate into our human costume, we forget where we have come from and who we really are. If you can imagine the complexities involved in a single life's plan, it is easy to see that free will, coupled with the amnesia we experience concerning who we really are, can cause us to stray from our original plan. However, despite our free will, we are always led back to our chosen path — even if the redirection process seems cruel and unabating at times.

We also choose the astrological timing of our birth. Astrologer Pam Gregory describes astrology as "the sacred language of divine intelligence." It helps us to understand the deeper meaning and purpose of our lives. Our birth chart is unique to us and will never be replicated. Thus, the alignment of the planets at the time of our birth play an important role and set the stage for the unfolding of our life's plan. The birth chart sets forth the patterns we will experience in our lifetime, as well as our potential; however, how we respond to these patterns as they play out in our life, and whether we reach our highest potential, will be dictated by our level of consciousness and the exercise of our free will.

The sun sign, the moon sign, ascendant, mid-heaven, and the moon's north and south nodes were all in the exact placement needed for us to live out the life we chose. The bigger picture of our life is revealed by the archetypal understanding and symbolism of the planets, the zodiac signs they rule (both the light and shadow sides), the elements, the genders, the aspects, and the houses they inhabited at the time of our birth. Within our natal birth chart lives an overview or snapshot of the blueprint of our soul's plan. As we live our life, we are influenced by our family, our culture, the larger society, and the events of the times in which we were born. As we grow and expand and continue to move forward on our journey, the planets themselves are also in constant movement. As they transit, they ignite or stimulate within us opportunities for growth. If we understand the language, we can use astrology as a tool or guidepost to better understand the influences or challenges we may be experiencing and the higher purpose behind them.

Knowing the birth chart of our spouse, we can understand the themes, patterns, and potentials they are meant to experience in their lifetime. With such knowledge, we can look more closely at their strengths and weaknesses, the areas in which they will likely shine, as well as details of their shadow side that are meant to be highlighted and healed during this incarnation. The more understand ourselves and those closest to us, the more we sharpen the lens of focus into our soul's higher purpose. We rarely search for a deeper meaning when we are experiencing events that bring us joy. However, for those events that introduce pain, confusion and change, astrology can be a good resource to help us understand the higher meaning and to evolve our consciousness as we move through the event or cycle.

## *Our Spirit Team / Guides*

From the moment we take our first breath, to the moment we shed our human costume, we have a team in spirit that is available to us during our lifetime. We never walk this journey alone; we have at least one main guide with us at every moment of our journey. This guide was involved in our pre-incarnation planning, and is therefore familiar with the details of our soul's plan and what we intended to accomplish in this lifetime. Our main guide is usually someone with whom we have had a previous life experience, and is matched to our soul's energetic make-up, our level of evolution, and what we are here to accomplish.

In addition to their familiarity with our current life plan, our main guides have a broader perspective of the totality of our soul's journey. They are familiar with the continuation of certain themes, talents, abilities, lessons, gifts, and contributions. They are familiar with the agreements or contracts we have with others, including the details of the more complicated contracts we have with those with whom we are traveling.

With such intimate knowledge of our life's plan and our purpose and predispositions, our guides are our best allies and support system during our sojourn on earth. They guide us, they nudge us when necessary, and even clear the path in front of us. Our guides mainly speak to us through our intuition. However, they also communicate with us through objective means and symbolic signs. Those who are clairaudient can hear their guides speak to them; those who are clairvoyant, can see them and/or the images they present; those who are clairsentient, can feel their presence; those who are claircognizant, can understand thought forms transferred to them by their guides.

Our guides will always find a way of communicating with us even when we are unconscious of their presence. When we need guidance, all we must do is ask. A guide will never interfere with our free will; as such, it is important that we do not assume they will prevent us from making a bad decision or from taking a certain action. A guide will always nudge us in the right direction and place opportunities in our path; however, the way we meet these opportunities will be governed by our free will. Additionally, the decisions we make — and the consequences of each decision — are ours alone. We will never be asked if we followed the guidance we received from our guides; we will, however, be asked if we followed our own wisdom. Helping us discover that wisdom is our guide's greatest virtue.

In addition to our main guide(s), we have others on our spirit team. They may be deceased loved ones, ancestors we have never known, or someone we have previously journeyed with; elementals and spirit animals also serve as guides. The spirit team assembled for a life's journey will be unique to each of us. Those who make up our spirit team are always available to us. One or more may be present, depending on our needs. If we need healing, we can ask for a healing guide to come and assist in our healing. If we need a certain teaching, we can ask for a teaching guide to come and assist in our learning. If we need inspiration, we may call in a guide to provide us the inspiration we need to continue. Whenever we ask for assistance, the guide best suited to meet our present need will be there. Just as we have family members, friends, colleagues, and associates with different talents, life experiences, knowledge, and specialties, we have an even richer base of willing participants in the spirit world.

The difference between the guidance we receive from those in spirit and that given by those souls currently living their human experience, is that we reap the benefit of the spirit guide's expanded perspective and lack of ulterior motives, as well as knowing that the guidance they share will always be for our highest good and the highest good of all involved. Yes, this does mean that we may not like the guidance we receive at times; however, it is our ego-mind that is resisting such a message. Once our ego and heart are aligned, the message will always have a peaceful resonance.

To ask for guidance, simply set the intention to receive the guidance, put out the call for assistance, and hold the knowing that your call will be received and responded to. Within your intention, be very clear that you are "only seeking guidance from a benevolent source from the light, and that the information you receive will be for your highest good and the highest good for all involved." My suggestion to protect yourself with your intention is not intended to induce fear; it is simply a reminder that we are beings among a vast multiverse, and we do not want to unknowingly open the door to beings who are not from the light. Once you have asked for guidance, release the request, and wait for an answer to come into your awareness. This is not the same concept as the familiar, "Let go and let God." We are in a true partnership with our guides; therefore, we must be willing to cooperate and do our part. We must be alert and watch for signs that may reveal our answer. An answer may come instantly or may take a little time. Be patient. An answer may be revealed in the words we read on a billboard, on a license plate, in a book or other written material we are inspired to read. It may be present in the words of a conversation we may have or might overhear, or perhaps in the lyrics of a song.

An answer might be revealed in a dream, while we are in a meditative state, walking, driving, or performing any mundane task throughout the day. Once we receive an answer, we must then act on the information we are provided for it to be of any use to us. Our guides will certainly make more than one attempt to reach us; however, it is important that we remain observant. Paying attention to what we are feeling, particularly around our solar plexus, is also important. We are certain to receive a "gut feeling," or knowing, the moment we hear or see something that is a direct response to our request. The first thought that comes into our awareness is usually the right answer. This is applicable to every area of our life, including divorce. It is only when we allow our logical mind to interfere with our knowing that we become doubtful.

When we need a simple yes or no response, we can ask our higher self to speak to us through the intelligence of our smart body, or simply communicate with our body directly. Set the intention in advance of how you desire your body to respond to you. Our bodies have a natural intelligence that is in constant communication with our consciousness. An example of a communication for the purpose of a yes or no response might include asking a question aloud, while standing in an upright position. A forward movement of the body following this inquiry might represent a "positive" response; and conversely, a backward movement of the body following the inquiry may represent a "negative" response. Some prefer to write the question on a piece of paper and hold the paper with both hands near the solar plexus, while asking their question aloud.

You may find that a simple relaxed feeling in the body represents a "positive" response for you, and a constricted feeling in the body represents a "negative" response. To set a communication pattern, begin by asking a few test questions that have definite "yes" or "no" responses to them. As an example, "Is my current name [insert your name]," and wait for a response. Then ask the same question using a name that is sure to receive a negative response, such as "Is my name Dumbo?," and wait for a response. After a few test questions, you will become familiar with how your body responds, both affirmatively and negatively.

You may find that making a statement such as, "My name is _____," may yield better results than using the question format. Many people find it helpful to use muscle testing (kinesiology) to set up a communication pattern with their body. Some find that using a pendulum or other divination tool for this purpose works better for them. Whatever method you choose, it should be a simple process developed by you, to be used by you. This does not require an elaborate system or extensive training.

In addition to our team of spirit guides who support our human journey, we must never forget that the larger part of our being — our light — our higher self, remains in the spirit world and works with us intimately, as well as collaboratively, with our team in spirit. When we incarnate into human form, we only bring a fragment or fractal of our light with us. The human body could never host the fullness of our light.

This fact might make the concept that we can be in more than one place at the same time more palatable. The larger part of us is blended with the light of all other souls in a collective union. There is no separation between us. Consciously building the metaphorical bridge to, and communing with, our higher self and spirit will begin to unfold the mystery of who we are, why we are here, and how we can begin to live a life that embodies our true essence.

## *Archangels*

Just as we would not send young children on a journey without appropriate chaperones, the Divine Source has blessed us with fifteen loving Archangels of pure light to watch over us, to protect us, to inspire us, and to provide advice and assistance to us along our journey. Archangels bring with them the unconditional love of the Divine Source, unlimited acceptance, and profound compassion. They cross all boundaries of space and time, and are available to all, regardless of religious beliefs, ideologies, and philosophies. They are messengers and helpers of the Divine Source, and each has unique virtues they sponsor.

The Archangels are aware of our divinity, the fullness of our soul, and our mission. With deep respect for our free will, they will never interfere with our choices, but will generously offer their assistance whenever we call upon them. Other than Archangel Metatron and his twin Archangel Sandalphon, the Archangels have not experienced life in human form. There are many guardian angels who work with us, both by request, and from behind the scenes. It is humans who have placed these lovely beings in a hierarchical structure and provided them with a rank, personality, and wings.

Angels are of the spirit; they are pure divine light. Therefore, they may appear to us in the form of a flash of light, or they may present themselves in a manner in which we have been taught to perceive them. For most, it is our faith and inner knowing that capture their essence when they make their presence known to us on a personal level. Even when we cannot perceive them at all, if our intentions are pure, know that they will be present.

Archangel Raguel, Archangel Zadkiel, and Archangel Michael are particularly valuable to those moving through divorce. Archangel Raguel is considered the Angel of Justice and Fairness. When we find ourselves in any dispute, Archangel Raguel may be called upon to intervene as a powerful mediator. He will help to summon truth from the parties to the dispute and will assist in an equitable outcome for the highest good of all involved. Archangel Zadkiel is considered the Archangel of Mercy and Benevolence. Archangel Zadkiel can be called upon to assist us with forgiving ourselves and forgiving another. He helps to widen our lens by bringing into our awareness the fullness, the milestones, the lessons, and the blessings on our journey. He can help us see a situation from different perspectives and encourage us to come into the situation from our divine nature with acceptance and compassion, which will bring peace into our heart.

Archangel Michael is the leader among the Archangels; and is the protector of the light of the Divine Source and the protector of all beings. Archangel Michael works with Ascended Master Saint Germaine, keeper of the divine violet flame, to alchemize lower energies that are sourced from fear into the divine light of love. Archangel Michael can be called upon to protect us from all things that bring us fear and are not sourced from the light. Call on him when you are feeling fearful or need protection and assistance from any negativity surrounding your divorce; ask that he bring you the courage of his warrior spirit, to help you proceed forward. *You can also make a simple request for the right angel to accompany you during all important phases of your divorce.*

## Ascended Masters

The Ascended Masters are highly evolved, enlightened, high-vibrational beings of love and light. Just as we are on a soul's journey of enlightenment and a return to the Divine Source, so too were the Ascended Masters. They experienced many lifetimes, and, through the progression of their souls' evolution, they mastered the principles of the Divine Source, evolved beyond the human karmic and rebirthing cycle, mastered the spiritual forces of the universe, and have fully blended with their divinity, their "I AM" presence. Ascended Masters are the prophets, saints and sages from all civilizations, cultures, religious and philosophical backgrounds who are united as the true wayshowers. They are here to assist each one of us with our own ascension. Some of the more well-known Ascended Masters include: Yeshua/Jesus, Moses, Buddha, Yogananda, Mother Mary, Saint Germaine, Saint Francis, Thoth, Moses, Babaji, Ganesh, Krishna, Lakshmi, Kuan Yin, White Tara, Portia, Merlin, Ashtar, Athena, Vesta, Serapis Bey, and Horus. You can call on any of these

Ascended Masters to assist you. They will be honored to respond to your call.

## The Author's Guide, "Chala"

My main guide, Chala, as is true for all of us, has been with me all my life. However, it was not until 2009 that I made a conscious effort to connect with her. During meditation or walks in nature, I would ask her to send me signs and to speak to me in a way so that I could hear and understand her. Eventually, I was able to hear her. In the beginning, it was just a few scattered words that made little sense. It was not long, however, before I was able to hear more clearly, and to see the symbolic images she conveyed with each sitting.

Although I can see spirits when I am engaged in mediumship, I remain unable to "see" Chala. There are also times when I am unable to connect and/or hear anything from Chala. It is then that I request her to speak to me through another medium. When Chala comes to share on my behalf, the medium is always stunned when they see her majestic presence and feel her powerful, yet loving, energy. I am reminded often that part of our soul's journey on earth is a walk of faith. We will never know all the answers, or what may be lurking in front of us; however, the more we work on building our faith, the more we are shown that it is through our faith that growth ensues. My absolute belief in, and relationship with, a guide I cannot see has helped to nurture my faith in many areas of my life — the most important being to trust myself.

What follows is a partial quote from the guidance I received from Chala concerning a personal relationship. I chose to share this quote to highlight the beautiful way our guides work with us. Their messages always come in love, and are devoid of judgment. They will often use metaphors we can understand that convey much more than the words they choose to share.

Our guides must use language, memories and other information within our subconscious to communicate with us; otherwise, we would be unable to decipher the message. This fact confuses many at the beginning of their journey, including myself, as it naturally feels as though our imagination is making up the words and symbols being shared. However, soon it becomes clear which thoughts are our own, as opposed to the thought patterns being conveyed from our guide(s).

This short quote emphasizes that the relationship was an important, pre-planned connection for my soul's journey; that we had a complicated, multiple-life contract together; that it was inevitable that synchronicity would bring us together; and that the contrast within the relationship had stimulated the lessons and blessings my soul intended to receive.

It was a thoughtful reminder that we have free choice in how we respond to contrasts in relationship. Prior to sharing her words, Chala shared an image wherein she handed me a bouquet of long-stemmed pink roses. As she placed the roses in my arms, I brushed my hand against them and cut my fingers on the thorns. She then stated:

*There is great beauty in the rose, is there not? And so, my child, with each rose comes thorns; and at times you bleed from the thorns. You are bleeding now. I ask you, child, if it is your fault that you are bleeding from the thorn, or is it simply that you have caressed the rose so deeply that you have bled? Thorns can be removed; it is a matter of choice as to whether they are. They are inherent in the rose, as they are in relationship. It is not that someone made a mistake in accepting the rose; it is rather the deep love of the rose that brings someone in contact with the thorns. It must be remembered that thorns are a choice. Loving the rose was never a choice; it was inherent in its fragrance that you would fall in love. I am Chala.*

In this instance, the spiritual contract between us was complete. However, the love increased between us with this understanding, and a lifelong friendship was established. We chose to rewrite our contract and to support each other's journey. Energetic cords were transformed rather than severed. It was later shared that our contract was indeed meant to last until one of us returns to the spirit world, and that we had traveled through many lifetimes together. The form and function of the relationship was our "choice." I would have missed years of my earthly sojourn without a member of my soul family, had my choice been different.

More than a year passed before Chala answered my request for a name by which I could refer to her. I chose the spelling to avoid any unintended interpretations. Despite my repeated requests for a name, Chala was very clear that those in spirit do not use names as a form of identification — their energy is their calling card. It was important to her that I was able to "feel" her presence. Our guides will, however, provide us with a name for our convenience.

Discovering Chala's presence, and then learning that she had always been with me, changed my life. My search for truth and understanding was accelerated. My commitment to engage in my own inner shadow work, although very difficult at times, was made easier with her guidance and unconditional love. I began doing the weeding of my own inner and outer gardens. I began re-erecting boundaries I had allowed to crumble; more importantly, I uncovered the events that precipitated this chain of reckless lack of self-care. I engaged in processes to alchemize and transmute the negative energy, sometimes repeatedly.

There remain events tucked away in my subconscious that will certainly surface in their own time. I was able to meet my own saboteur face-to-face and discover why this archetypal energy was present. True to the cliché, "A bad penny always shows up," my saboteur remains an unwanted guest at times. However, my acknowledgment and response time has quickened with each of his visits. There will always be more layers to discover about ourselves, no matter how much hard work we do. Nevertheless, understanding why we are here, what we are meant to learn and accomplish while we are here, and, that we are not operating alone, makes the journey far richer and tames our human tendency to resist challenges rather than embracing them.

## *Spirit Helpers in the Author's Divorce*

Many guides have come and gone to assist me on my own journey, even when I was unconscious of their presence; there was no mistaking the influence and assistance I received during these encounters.

When it came time for my own divorce, I was nudged to get out, fast. I was in my second year of law school, and our income came from working together. When I announced my intention to leave, my husband emptied all the bank accounts. While I was in class, he contacted an upscale secondhand store to clear our residence of everything — except my clothes and the contents of my daughter's bedroom. He told me, "We came here with ten boxes, and that is what we'll leave with!" He sent defamatory letters to my mother, my friends and the Dean of the law school.

Within a few days, I was summoned to his attorney's office to sign a marital settlement agreement. Despite the fact that I was in law school and therefore understood that my legal rights would be affected, I signed the settlement agreement without reading it, and immediately left the building. Unable to secure a rental property as a self-employed student, and with no funds remaining in the bank accounts or in my handbag, I surrendered. I lay on my bed, closed my eyes, and cried as I prayed for higher guidance.

Mysteriously, somehow I knew I was protected and would be provided for, I just did not know how. I continued to pray for guidance and fought back the fear that had perched on my shoulders like a lead weight. After several days, I drove by a newer condominium building that I passed by several times a week, and immediately felt a strong nudge to stop in the complex. Although I questioned, "Why am I looking at a condominium in an expensive zip code, when I couldn't possibly secure a mortgage?," I parked my car, took a deep breath, and walked into the sales office.

We are not to question the "how" of what we receive, we are simply to follow the guidance. A nice young woman greeted me and happily showed me two available units. Feeling rather ashamed as we walked through one of the units, I shared my current situation with this lovely young woman and made this bold statement: "I just need someone to believe in me."

Although I left the property feeling anxious, as I drove home, I started imagining what it would be like to live in the upper unit at the condominium, which had plenty of square footage, and a view of maple trees from every window. It felt as though I was in a tree house. It was, of course, the more expensive unit, so it was not long before my doubt took over and I dismissed the idea as an impossibility. To my surprise, I received a telephone call later that same evening from the young woman who showed me the two units. With excitement in her voice, she informed me that her father was the builder of the complex and his company also provided financing. When she shared my story with her father, he told her, "No problem; offer her a nine-day close, with a low initial adjustable interest rate mortgage, and a down payment of nine thousand dollars; that should do it."

Interestingly, one of the symbolic meanings of the number nine in numerology is transition, the end of one cycle and the beginning of another. I accepted this offering with gratitude; however, as soon as the call was disconnected, I began to panic again: "How am I going to make this happen in nine days? Where is the money going to come from?"

I again surrendered. As soon as I settled down in my bed for the night, a clear vision of my lifelong friend from my hometown in California began nudging me like an alarm I could not shut off. I went out to the backyard and called him. Within two days, this angel gifted me with nine thousand dollars, wired directly to the escrow company. Although I moved to this property with just my clothes, the contents of my daughter's bedroom, a lawn chair, artwork, and the few antiques the consignment store did not take, I never felt so abundant and safe. Even the fact that my conscious mind was struggling with how I could complete law school and take care of expenses on just student loans — and whatever work my husband and I could continue to do together, if any — I knew I was safe and free.

My divorce was not processed for some time; however, there was nothing to argue, fight or be passionate about — because our settlement agreement was already signed. He was the stepfather to my daughter, and I wanted the scope and quality of their relationship to be guided by them. I knew our time together as husband and wife had come to an end. During my later inner soul work on this relationship, I understood the terms of the soul contract between me and my husband. Soul contracts will be discussed in the next chapter. The deeper I searched, the more I understood the experiences that rendered the contract complete. In fact, I learned the contract was completed a few years prior to my leaving.

Perhaps my inner archetypal abandoned child needed time to gather the strength to take the leap of faith. It is interesting that the day we were married, my husband said to me, "You know, this is only good for ten years." Did his statement come from some inner knowing? Was he led to make the statement so that I would have a physical marker to reflect upon at the time I took the steps to dissolve the marriage? It was during the eighth year that I announced my departure.

I will, of course, have to wait to learn the answer to these questions; but the overall experience presents a good example of how our path is not easy, nor is it easy to understand what the higher meaning might be, at the time we are experiencing a certain event. I have communicated my gratitude to my former husband for the role he played in my soul's development. We have since discussed, cried, forgiven and acknowledged the blessings we each contributed to the other. Although I would have appreciated this higher understanding at the time I was experiencing this transition, it is never too late to seek understanding, to forgive, to receive forgiveness if such is offered, and to show compassion to yourself and to the other party. The dance may be clumsy, but as soon as we learn the lessons and make atonement where necessary, the lessons are cleared from our curriculum.

By sharing a glimpse into my own experience, I am not suggesting that you travel as blindly through your divorce process as I did. However, I am suggesting that you have a team in spirit that is there to work with you, has your back, and will provide you with needed guidance. As soon as we take the first step toward breaking a pattern and moving forward on our journey, our higher self and our spirit team are always available to provide us with a perceptional view far beyond our earthbound understanding. When our intentions are clear, the divine universe begins manipulating the energy and clears the path for us to proceed. Synchronistic events, people and resources come to us without much effort beyond maintaining our faith and keeping our vibration as high as we can throughout the process. We simply must be willing to ask to be shown the truth — our truth, and be equally willing to digest and process the answers we are provided.

We are in control of the actions we take; however, it is reassuring to know that our decisions will be based upon our higher truth even if it brings pain or confusion to us at the time we are making a choice. Whenever we feel as though we are losing something, be it a person, a thing, an employment or career opportunity, a way of life, or even a marriage, we must have faith that the person or thing we are "losing" is not a vibrational match to our future self. Whether something is taken from us before we are ready to set it free, or we have been nudged to consciously set it free ourselves, there are no mistakes. Rather than viewing such a loss as an empty space, we are called to trust that what is happening is for our highest good and that the space will be filled with treasure gifted from our soul.

It is our humanness that cries out for understanding while our soul sings with excitement for what is to come. If we could settle into this understanding during a time of transition, we would avoid the need to experience the fear and worry that accompanies major life shifts. We would have an inner knowing that we will always be provided for, that we are always guided to the next step on our journey, and most importantly, that we never walk alone. May you begin to feel your higher self, your spirit team, and the benevolent Divine Source surrounding you now like a warm blanket.

We must never forget that after a dark night comes light — we must always look toward the light. When our shadow beckons us to move backward, we must continue to put one foot in front of the other. I want to put your mind at ease that the idea of spending hours and hours working with and dissecting our shadow side is not necessarily a process we must endure. So long as our intentions are pure and we are not resisting our shadow but are actively seeking the lessons and blessings from our experiences, we gain the *jewels of wisdom* much quicker, and the process is more streamlined. There is no longer a need to dig to the depths of each trauma from our childhood and other life events and lifetimes in order to clear the energy and heal.

As we move further into the Aquarian Age, the cause and effect, or "karma" of our past experiences will no longer be the method of choice to assist in our evolutionary growth.

However, to truly evolve from this cycle, we must each capture the wisdom of our experiences — or else we will remain in this cycle for some time. We are each at different stages of our evolutionary journey. Wisdom for some may surface instantaneously; for others, it may take further excavation before they capture the wisdom required to completely heal and release. There is no magic pill, ceremony, or ritual that will implant the wisdom our soul needs to evolve. To achieve true healing, and to avoid the consequences of engaging in a spiritual bypass (a phrase coined in 1984 by American Psychologist John Welwood to describe using spiritual ideas and practices in order to avoid facing unresolved emotional issues or psychological wounds), we must be present and willing to do the work our soul is requesting of us. If we avoid what is surfacing within us, we miss its higher purpose.

We must be present when we are triggered, and use our discernment as it relates to what we need. Avoidance keeps the shadow energy in our field and is a clear invitation for the universe to bring us another similar event to stimulate our learning. Similarly, the concept that we can simply take a large eraser and wipe the slate clean is wishful thinking. We have already walked through the experiences; a brief look back from the perspective of our higher self, as the observer without attachment, will reveal the wisdom we need to move forward. We will walk lighter, as the wisdom of the light is easier to carry than the denseness of our woundedness. We also create space for new experiences to enter without a karmic attachment. If we allow ourselves to engage in the process and seek the assistance we need, we will all evolve together sooner into the promised higher understanding and harmony of the Aquarian Age.

It is important for us to remember that, as we are healing and releasing what no longer serves us, we are also assisting others on the path with us, those who have come before us, as well as those who are yet to come. Consequently, they too will experience the healing, release and freedom from the karmic cycles that have enslaved us. What we do for ourselves matters and has an impact. The more self-love, compassion, and forgiveness we can give to ourselves, the greater the impact we will have on others. The quickening of the energy surrounding the alchemy process of healing does not mean that we can become complacent. We must capture and collect the *jewels of wisdom* from our encounters if we wish to avoid slipping back into the cause-and-effect patterns from which we are slowly emerging. Free choice remains — we must remain diligent and use it wisely.

# 14

# The Role of Relationships and Soul Contracts

## *Relationships*

Our relationships are the mirrors to our soul. We learn about ourselves and grow from observing and seeing ourselves in the reflection of those with whom we engage. From a simple encounter with a stranger, to our most intimate relationships, what we admire in another reflects an attribute that we also possess and are invited to share and experience. In these moments of recognition, our higher self is highlighting the beauty and pure love within us. The moment we feel a compassionate, accepting, non-judgmental gesture from another, whether it be through the spoken word or in a simple non-verbal behavior, we are reminded of our own inner truth, and our frequency rises in response to this recognition. Similarly, when the behavior of another individual triggers us to experience hurt, betrayal, jealousy, defensiveness, anger, resentment, and other such fear-centered emotions, that conduct too is a mirror exposing an area within us that needs our attention. The intensity of our reaction to a trigger is a direct indication of the intensity of that attribute that lives within us, as well as our own propensity to inflict the same behavior upon another. Rarely do we take the opportunity when we have been triggered to ask, "What is this experience trying to teach or reveal to me?" It is a typical response to either lash out toward an individual who triggers us, or to withdraw and hide our own power under a layer of shame, guilt, or other similar emotion. When we proceed through a divorce without awareness, this tendency is likely to be magnified.

It has been said that when we point our finger in blame towards another person, three fingers remain in our own direction. If we think back to how many times we have been triggered to feel a certain emotion from one or more individuals, we can begin to pull the curtain back and reveal the lesson or blessings from these encounters. We begin to capture our soul's intended higher purpose. If we find we are triggered over and over, it is a clear indication that the repeat button has been pushed because we are missing the higher truth from the experience. When we allow ourselves to open the inquiry and pay homage to the lesson or blessing that is there for us to uncover, the need for that form of stimulus leaves our energy field. We no longer need to attract similar experiences.

The space is then opened to be filled with new experiences that bring us joy, peace, abundance, and freedom. We are not here to simply host a repeated number of uncomfortable experiences. As souls, we are free, our natural state is one of peace; we are meant to be abundant in every area of our life. If we can consciously move through the curriculum of those experiences that are meant to foster our soul's evolution, we will have more time to enjoy and experience the extracurricular experiences we choose to co-create.

The more intimate the relationship, the more we are called to stretch and to open, and to see ourselves in the eyes of another. Our most intimate relationships hold the key to the lessons and understandings our soul incarnated into this lifetime to learn and master. If we can adjust our vision so that we can review our relationships as an observer, that is, from that all-knowing part of us that carries great wisdom — our higher self — we would intentionally set aside the hurt, the feelings of betrayal, the anger, and any other emotion that has surfaced out of the energy of fear, and is preventing us from experiencing the clarity we seek. It is from this space that we make quantum leaps in our spiritual development.

To truly heal, alchemize and transmute what we perceive to be the negative transgressions against us, we must be willing to open the box from a detached perspective and dive in deeper — until the nuances catch our attention, and we begin to see colors and patterns that have repeated themselves time and time again. When we take this brave journey into the self, it becomes very clear that, if the behavior of another individual triggers us, it is focusing on an energy within ourselves that needs our love, our own forgiveness, our compassion, acceptance, and the freedom of release. With some issues, we can accomplish this process in a manner of minutes. With more significant issues, it may take more time; but once we set the intention to heal and focus our attention in that direction, we are instantly surrounded with the guidance we need.

## *Soul Contracts / Agreements*

With the understanding that our soul has a plan for this lifetime, it is imperative that we take a deeper look at the agreements or contracts we have with other souls who are sojourning and engaging with us. Using my own experience as an example, if I entered into a soul contract or agreement with my father to be born into his union with my mother, then it would behoove me to understand the underlying lessons my soul intended to receive from the experience. I was born twenty-two years into my parents' marriage, and I was the only child. My father was sick with heart and kidney disease during my childhood, and returned to the spirit world when I was nine years of age. Interestingly, the number nine appears as it later did with my divorce, symbolizing the ending of a cycle and the beginning of a new cycle.

Despite my desperate pleas against it, I was forced to be a "good little girl," and sit beside my mother in the first row of the Catholic memorial service, with my father's open casket right in front of me. During the veterans' ceremonial service that followed, I stood there, frozen, with the piercing sound of Taps playing in the air. But being the good little girl that I was, I just silently screamed in fear as they lowered my father's casket into the dark, hollow ground. My mother was traumatized by the loss of my father, and experienced many months of depression and hospitalization after his death.

We can glean from this life event that one of my key soul lessons of this lifetime is to understand and overcome the archetype of the abandoned child. Moreover, this experience fostered a belief in me that I was *not* supported, that it is *not* acceptable for me to speak my truth, that I am *not* free to erect boundaries for my self-protection, and that I *cannot* trust men or women to have my best interests at heart. Clearly, this is an interesting paradigm, based upon the illusion of fear.

I feel it important to note that my mother had three sisters, who each had large families living within a thirty-minute drive of where my mother and I lived. However, I was not embraced in the arms of a "loving family" when my mother spent months in a hospital. Instead, I was bounced around among family friends, resulting in my exposure to a less-than-scenic tour of the dark side of the adult world. This lack of concern and interest from the larger family demonstrates to me that the soul contract between us was crafted to support my soul's intended journey through this period — that I was meant to walk this time alone, while the paradigm that would influence all my future experiences was locked firmly into place. Isolation, mistrust, fear, and a call for self-reliance took over every cell of my body.

With the energy of the abandoned child fueling my tank, it is not surprising that I became a reckless and rebellious pre-teen and teenager. I walked away from the Catholic Church by refusing to attend my confirmation, and making the blanket statement that the church "is full of *hit." Had my father been alive at the time, I am sure I would have been knocked back into submission rather quickly. By the age of fifteen, I had become a mother myself and set-up housekeeping with my daughter's father. Not surprisingly, the young relationship did not last past my eighteenth birthday, although we have remained friends throughout the years. I completed high school by enrolling in a teen mother program during my pregnancy, and received a GED rather than a high school diploma. I was determined to be a "good mother" and a "good influence," although I am not sure what I thought that would be like at the time — considering that I was raising myself as well as my daughter.

I made a firm commitment, however, to complete my education. Without my initiation into a life of perseverance and determination, my fate might have turned out differently. I think of my daughter as my blessing of grace, who came into my life at just the right time. However, we know that there are no mistakes, and that we too, were fulfilling our contractual agreements with each other.

In an ironic twist of fate, I attended Marymount College at the start of my journey and was accepted by the Catholic University Columbus School of Law for graduate school. The very organization that I had walked away from became my lifeline to completing my educational goals. Although I never returned to the Catholic faith, I learned a life-long lesson, to always remain neutral. Attachment to or against any one belief will knock us out of alignment with our own truth. Whenever we find ourselves needing to defend or fight against something, it is a sign to take a pause, go within, and realign. In a world of duality, there are no absolutes; truths and falsehoods are present everywhere.

I started my study of world religions and philosophies during my time at Marymount College, and learned to appreciate them for their central core messages. I had to come back to my own familiar paradigm in some capacity, however, to be able to thoughtfully expand my lens of understanding. This experience ignited my spiritual journey and my search for truth.

The circumstances surrounding my father's death, which triggered many events that followed me well into my adult life, have given me opportunities to recognize and acknowledge the presence of the abandoned child within me. From it, I have grown, stretched my heart's capacity and, eventually, forgiven my father for his early departure from this earth, forgiven my mother for leaving me to fend for myself, and forgiven myself for the times I have projected this experience onto others.

My mother's own mother died shortly after giving birth to her, and mother was adopted and raised by an aunt. Although a family member took her in, mother shared my experience of being an abandoned child. My father passed away when mother and father were both in their 50s. As a single mother raising a small child, mother's abandoned child was triggered, and triggered again, when I left home at the age of fifteen, much sooner than she had expected me to leave.

Once I looked back at this scenario with compassion, I could clearly see that my mother did the best she could at the time. She was also on her own journey of learning and expanding. I came later into mother's life, and my daughter came into mine very early. However, despite our mistakes, we both did the best we could with the tools we had available.

Healing from this one event has been a long journey. As soon as I think I have mastered it, I have another experience that again revives the energy of the abandoned child. We must accept that some events in our life are harder than others to alchemize into expressions of wisdom; yet we keep moving forward, trusting that we will eventually graduate from the learning and perhaps even teach and assist another based on our experience.

It was hard for me to accept this fact, and to find the place within me that now treasures this life event for the gifts and wisdom it has provided to me. It deepens my healing each time I am triggered as well as each time I can sprinkle out wisdom to a fellow traveler experiencing similar circumstances.

## *Soul Contract / Agreement between Spouses*

Like our relationship with our parents, there is no greater platform for exploring the intended lessons of our soul's journey than through our relationship with a spouse. Making the investment to do the inner work with the intention of understanding the relationship from a soul's perspective, and asking the question, "What is the contract/agreement we share, and has that contract been completed?" is all we need to do to initiate the process. It is important to recognize those times in the relationship when we played the role of the teacher and held up a mirror for our spouse to consider, and those times when we were on the receiving end, as the student, with the mirror facing in our direction. Did we push away the mirror with the force of our ego, or did we use these opportunities to go within and discover and uncover those shadow pieces within us that were being highlighted?

Setting aside the behavior, or the issue that was surfacing because of the behavior, long enough to analyze the message will ignite our soul's learning and bring us the clarity we seek. This applies to experiences in which either spouse triggered moments of upliftment and encouragement in the other, as well as moments of pain. All events, from the most mundane to the most extreme, disclose a deeper story. Our relationships are all layered with richness. In the moments of reviewing the relationship from the perspective of the observer, you will begin to see the contract unfold as though the words are lifted from the page and spoken directly to your heart. If our spouse, or anyone else, triggers anger in us, it is a clear indication that we harbor anger within ourselves that needs our attention. This anger may not be related to the specific issue that has triggered it. Our propensity to *feel* anger is what the mirror is reflecting to us. It is for us to discover why the anger is present.

This exercise is not being suggested for the purpose of salvaging the marriage; rather, it is meant to provide us with a deeper understanding of ourselves, and areas within us that are wounded and need our attention. We can see how we show up in our intimate relationships, and how our past experiences and belief systems influence the ways we take in and digest certain information.

Moreover, this exercise explains (1) our responses and behavioral patterns, (2) how we care or fail to care for ourselves, (3) when we have yielded our power to our spouse, and (4) why. It helps us to heal; not just from the patterns of the marriage, but from a lifetime (and perhaps lifetimes) of experiencing the same patterns without a final resolution. This helps us to put an end to the "vicious" cycle and ultimately, sets us free. Viewing the relationship from the perspective of our higher self neutralizes every aspect of the marital relationship. We have the power to lift the veil concealing higher understanding and proceed forward with the divorce from the clear vantage point of our soul.

The issue of infidelity is one of the more difficult challenges to work through in a divorce; yet it leads to intense self-reflection for the parties involved. Focusing our attention on the person who suddenly learns about his or her spouse's infidelity, we can understand why he or she may feel hurt, not good enough, disrespected, angry, vengeful, even abandoned — emotions that are all based in fear.

If we remove the act of infidelity from the equation, we can then ponder the question, "What are the messages, issues or woundedness that may be surfacing now for this individual?" With some excavation, we might discover that he or she has either knowingly — or unknowingly — abandoned their own self-worth. Perhaps they have lost respect for themselves. They may have lowered their boundaries over time — or even failed to erect them in the first place. With this realization, the spouse on the receiving end of the infidelity may feel inspired to finally step out of fear and begin the resurrection of boundaries, rather than engage further with anger, incrimination, or other negative responses that may be surfacing.

He or she may finally see through the illusion and be able to answer the clarion call of their soul, perhaps even be motivated to search for, and finally find, the true source of their woundedness. Then, and only then, can the "victimized" spouse begin to own and integrate that aspect of themselves fully — so completely that he or she might eventually (and figuratively) take the hand of their own inner wounded child and lovingly let that child know that he or she is worthy, safe, self-reliant, and absolutely deserving of loving relationships with, and respect from, others.

By the intentional acceptance, love and integration of these aspects of themselves, the spouse can finally perform his or her own spiritual alchemy — using the power of their own love to transform the density of the lower vibration of their woundedness into the higher vibration of their divine nature.

The betrayed spouse may even discover that the contract with their spouse has been completed for some time, but that it took the act of infidelity to bring the marriage to a formal end. The more subtle signposts and nudges that were missed along the way may finally be recognized, painful as they are. The betrayed spouse might be able to stretch his or her understanding even more, recognizing that there are no mistakes. Their spouse might just have a contract with his or her paramour involved in the infidelity; and, perhaps the injured spouse, although unaware in his or her human shoes, may have been a party to the preincarnation planning of this life event.

As painful as that might be, it does certainly elicit a change in perception. The party on the receiving end of the infidelity might discover, in time, that he or she was destined to travel with another partner during this lifetime — and that the new relationship was synchronistically made possible because of the dissolution of the current marriage. An individual who comes into our life is meant to travel with us in some capacity. Some experiences with these soul travelers are wonderfully divine; others bring pain and/or unwanted change into our lives.

When we allow our soul the opportunity to truly communicate with us, we often find that a difficult event we are experiencing is actually for our highest good — even if we cannot find the reason why, at the time.

The individuals whom I have represented on the receiving end of infidelity are usually consumed with feelings of anger, resentment, despair, sadness, fear, and have fully embraced the role of the victim. However, those who have agreed to engage in the analysis described earlier in this chapter, for themselves, were able to take back their power, re-construct their boundaries, find the wounds within them and master the steps to healing. They were able to build a bridge of co-parenting with their spouse, if children were involved, and move into their future without carrying with them the burdens, negative emotions, and self-judgment surrounding the infidelity.

These clients were able to continue their deep inner work, even as they moved forward with anticipation and a healthy sense of closure. It was no longer important for them to dig for the reasons for the infidelity, or to want to exact revenge for their spouse's behavior. It was enough for them to know that they had gathered the *jewels of wisdom* from the experience, acknowledged and healed the energy within that needed attention, and listened to their inner knowing that it was time to move forward.

From this space on, the energy of dealing with divorce pivoted dramatically for these individuals. They were able to swiftly reach an amicable settlement agreement, as if all the pieces had divinely fallen into place.

It is not for us to assess, judge, or feel responsible for, whether our spouse used, or will use in the future, the mirrors of self-reflection we presented to them. Each person is on an individual journey. Although we are always charged with assisting others, we can never do the work on someone else's behalf. If an individual chooses to sit it out on a bench of indifference and/or denial, our job is, nevertheless, done. It is our responsibility to attend to our own growth, learning and understanding. The more we look, the more we will expose the clear, and sometimes mysterious, nuances of the lessons we came here to learn. With a simple shift of perspective, we can set aside our desire to blame, shame or punish the party who was responsible for bringing opportunities for growth to the surface, and instead, we can view their behavior as the completion to a provision in our soul contract. This is not to suggest that this is an easy process, or that we are meant to condone bad behavior. It is, however, an enlightened way of stepping out of the illusion of our perceived reality and graduating from the experience with a certificate of soulful completion.

The more we are triggered by an event, the more serious is the issue or lesson we are being called upon to address. Just as a mother's call to her children to come indoors at dusk becomes louder and louder with each attempt, we will discover that the behavior triggering us has similarly intensified over time — due to our own indifference, denial, and, unfortunately, the fact that we often cast ourselves in the role of victim.

Once we commit to the process of exploring those areas within us from the perch of our higher knowing, and, with an eye on our soul's journey — the waves of understanding, acknowledgement, and forgiveness to ourselves and others bring a refreshing awareness and a sense of peace. This unexpectedly elicits a sort of gratitude to the party who allowed us to finally see with clarity, even though our human heart and ego may wish to hold on to pain, anger and disappointment a bit longer.

As we begin to review all our relationships from this perspective, we can then more clearly see the roles we play for one another. Some are brief cameos, some are life-long assignments, and some are somewhere in between those two. Whatever time we have together, we are all mirrors for each other. No matter how well we play our roles, we are all on a higher mission to assist one another on our soul's journey. Even when our conscious mind is unaware of the depth of the challenge, we are always hard at work for each other. We begin to naturally reflect when we acknowledge the times we failed to look within, and how those choices were our invitations for the experience to resurface yet again. Therefore, it behooves us to take the challenge — even when we are at our weakest and most vulnerable. Our heart-space, that area within us that connects us to our true essence, is more easily accessed, and is always ready to welcome us, when we enter with integrity and pure intentions.

## *When Inner Work is Left Undone*

If not properly processed, the internal pain, hurt, anger, resentment, regret, shame, and feelings of betrayal either party experienced during the marriage itself and/or the divorce process, will remain and will almost certainly follow them into their next relationship. Friendships and work-related relationships may also be affected.

The feeling that one is not safe will remain imprinted like a tattoo on the heart. If the dissolution of the relationship is not seen as a means of looking deeply within the self, we will simply attract another partner with the same attributes. A seemingly brand-new and shiny relationship will often offer exactly the same patterns, belief systems and insecurities as the earlier relationships.

These aspects will have another opportunity to be exposed. The need to learn and expand remains a catalyst for future experiences that will trigger the opportunities to facilitate this expansion. A different face and even a different place will not obviate the need to fulfill our soul's mission. Under these circumstances, the mirror that is held up by a new love will most certainly have an enhanced magnification.

If we are not successful in mastering the lessons or issues presented to us during our divorce, the stakes of the next relationship, in terms of our learning, are higher. It is a well-known statistic that the probability of divorce increases with a second or third marriage. In terms of timeline, if we miss the boat of knowing how to expand in a relationship and simply continue to sail with the same wind speed and in the same direction as in the earlier marriage, we will gradually navigate ourselves into rougher and rougher waters.

As an attorney, it is disappointing to have a former client return to initiate his or her second, third or sometimes, fourth divorce. The patterns that were present in the prior relationship(s) can clearly be seen to be playing out again in the current relationship. The circumstances surrounding a new relationship trigger the same wounded aspects within us, until the shield of victimhood is removed. Then, feeling naked and raw, the focus of the microscope is turned inward.

Emotion by emotion, pattern by pattern, event after event, we are awakened, and pay a long-overdue visit to areas within us that are ripe for healing. After being encouraged to search for the root cause of each expression, we provide that wound with a voice so it will be acknowledged, loved, fully integrated and alchemized into our highest expression of love. In so doing, we give the inner child within us the love, respect, dignity and understanding that he or she needs — and has been waiting patiently for, through multiple relationships and/or experiences. Self-parenting our inner child is the most loving thing we can do for ourselves. From this space, our intention to transmute and release the negative energy is manifested by a stream of divine cleansing love.

If we can view our important relationships in terms of the long journey — the many lifetimes we may have shared, and the multiple roles we may have played for each other — we begin to widen the scope even further. We can assume that our spouse has been cast in the role of our parent, our child, our sibling, our best friend, or perhaps a comrade in a war. We experience both the female and male energies as our predominant human expression; and, we have been, or may be, wearing a female or male costume while experiencing the opposite energy as our predominant expression in this lifetime. One of the pleasures we receive as a soul living in a temporary human costume is the experience of human emotion. All of us are on a journey to be united with the Divine Source. We are all traveling through multiple timelines, exploring and learning, stumbling and inspiring, to discover the true essence of who we are, and to be reunited with the wholeness of divine love.

Love is the goal of the journey. We experience human love that serves as an elixir, a drug, a master of trickery and illusion. In our search for the understanding and experience of unconditional love, we dance and play with the spectrum of every emotion in the human experience. Using our free will, coupled with our conditioning, programming, and the stories we create and believe in, we pick and choose from the buffet of options available to us.

At times, the mind begins to distort what the soul is trying to communicate, and we begin making choices from a place of disempowerment. Food, drug, alcohol and shopping addictions, lying, codependency, and other destructive behaviors are birthed out of a strong need to avoid the inner walk over the bridge where the mind and higher self are connected. We continue to look outward rather than within, because we are afraid of coming face-to-face with what is hiding within us. We are invited to greet our inner beast from our higher place of knowing, our observation point, without attachment, and with courage — not fear. If we are willing to turn within, to place our hand upon the head of the beast with tenderness and compassion, we will notice an immediate softening, a recognition of that innocent, younger part of our self that has been waiting to be reunited. When we resist, we allow the beast the freedom to continue to roam within us until it finds a new form of expression. Accordingly, it is inevitable that we will be triggered again and again. New experiences will always be presented by the soul, to trigger and send a reminder of what is yet to be discovered.

The light within us is untouched by our earthly experience and shines as brightly as the sun's glare on the surface of the ocean. When we free ourselves, we learn that the wingspan of our light is endless, and is connected to the unconditional divine light of our source — no barriers, no conditions, no rules of engagement, just pure, unconditional love. If we can anchor ourselves to this understanding, we can see the illusion and the play we are engaged in.

We recognize that all souls currently living on this earthly stage, or who have retired their human costume — as well as the souls from all other dimensions, past, present and future — are connected to us and we are connected to them. We get a peek backstage and learn that we are all expressions of the Divine Source, and that we are all engaged in co-creating our individual and collective expressions and experiences. What a blessing we give ourselves when we begin to view ourselves and our fellow travelers from this perspective.

We chose to experience the world of duality in human form and to begin our incarnation with a form of amnesia. It is equally our choice to break through the illusion; this can be accomplished through courage and the willingness to excavate deep enough within ourselves to find the light that embodies our true essence, but has been buried within the clutter of our human experience.

It is not until we remove the veil of illusion, welcome in who we really are, and disavow all contracts, paradigms, beliefs and behaviors that do not serve our own highest good, that we will realize we have been waiting for someone or something outside of ourselves to hear us, to see us, to acknowledge our pain, our sacrifices, and to, somehow, make it all better. During a divorce, these tendencies can be amplified. Taking control and ending this cycle is not a selfish act; in fact, it is the most selfless action we can take. When we serve our own highest good, we are serving the highest good of everyone we encounter. The more our awareness expands, the more we must remain firm in our commitment to care for ourselves, to show compassion to ourselves, and to love ourselves. Once we can show the love to ourselves that we crave from others, we lose the need to search for love outside of ourselves. Our elusive relationship to love is transformed. As we re-erect our boundaries and treat ourselves with respect and dignity, and we honor our own integrity, so too will others. Loving ourselves wholly — our raw and beautiful selves — not simply pacifying our wounded selves, is essential to releasing us from years of needless bondage.

# 15

# The Fragmented Soul and Deep Healing

With every traumatic experience, we leave a fragment of our soul essence behind. If we were bullied on the school playground, rejected for a team, physically and/or emotionally abused, heartbroken from a first love, or experienced any other traumatic event, a fragment of our soul was left abandoned and anchored there, in that space. Moreover, we may have abandoned fragments of our soul after traumas experienced in other lifetimes. As we proceed through life, and experience additional pains, losses, fears, shame, grief, embarrassment, disappointment, or when we make decisions that were induced by the pressure from others rather than from our own inner guidance, we can become extremely fragmented. With this understanding, it is no wonder that we find ourselves searching for a sense of wholeness, why at times we feel incomplete, numb, or apathetic, and why we might experience gaps in our memory, unexplained fears, feelings of depression and alienation, and even manifest illness. An individual experiencing trauma associated with their divorce may be susceptible to soul fragmentation. They may have an inability to let go of the relationship and unknowingly attach a firm grip on a piece of their spouse's soul. It may be their spouse who is unable to let go of the relationship and they may experience a similar attachment.

While our modern medical community attempts to sooth our symptoms using pharmaceutical treatments, traditional Shamans of ancient civilizations had a firm understanding that we are each a soul, and that the soul of a person must be attended to if true healing is to take place. This holistic approach implemented sacred practices and rituals that included the retrieval of splintered soul fragments. The work of a traditional Shaman was a lifelong commitment, and required years of apprenticeship under the tribe's elder Shaman. Among other ritualistic practices, a Shaman journeyed to the spirit world, and with the help of animal totems and other guides, collected an individual's soul fragments so that alignment, balancing, and the connection to the individual's true essence could be restored. Many cultures continue this practice within the purity of their ancestral traditions. Anthropologist Michael Harner brought the practice of Shamanic healing to the modern world through his Foundation for Shamanic Studies. I have attended workshops from this foundation as well as other organizations. In addition to learning the traditions and practices, the knowledge I gained about myself from these experiences was just as valuable. Many modern healers undertake arduous training and years of study to be certified as Shamanic Healers. They can be a good resource for the purpose of soul retrieval, as well as offering other healing services. I have had the privilege of two healing sessions with traditional Shamans, and the experience was undeniably healing.

Energy healing modalities such as Reiki, Qigong, Therapeutic Touch Therapy, Access Bars, the use of light, sound or magnets, and many other modalities are good resources. Learning EFT Tapping is a good option for self-treating the stress and anxiety associated with divorce. Transpersonal hypnotherapy, and other hypnotherapy methods such as Quantum Healing Hypnosis Technique (QHHT), are good modalities for both soul fragment retrieval, as well as assisting in the discovery of the root cause of specific issues. It is important to note that the "healer" acts as a bridge between us, our higher self, and our helpers in the spirit world.

Whether the healer acts as a conduit for the energy exchange or as a facilitator to assist our communication with our higher self and our guides in a hypnotherapy session, we are the ones who ultimately provide our own healing. It is our belief, our intention, and the intention of our higher self that determines the level of healing and the information that is to be shared. Accordingly, it is important to access where you are in terms of your beliefs and your willingness to attend a healing session with the right intention, and an openness that will allow you to receive rather than to resist. It is the job of our ego to protect us from harm, and it will always try to bring out our skepticism and doubt. If you are attracted to a particular healing modality or practitioner, trust your intuition, and make a conscious effort to put your ego mind at ease. Remind your ego that you are partners on the healing journey, and that it is safe for your ego to take a break and just stand by and observe.

Our higher self knows exactly what we need for our spiritual growth. Many clients have discovered former lifetimes they have experienced with their current spouse, and even with the children of their marriage. Learning that the main players in our life are a part of our larger soul group, and that our travels together may be extensive, naturally brings a level of understanding, peace, and healing. Depending on where we are on our spiritual journey, the initial learning of this information can be confusing; however, it ultimately serves to broaden the perspective of our current relationships and allows us to move forward with a knowing that these relationships are timeless and serve a higher purpose.

There are many gifted mental health professionals who can assist an individual through the transition of divorce. If you are currently seeing a therapist, you are encouraged to continue with your sessions. Mental health professionals can provide not only a safe place to share and talk through the story of the marriage and the divorce process, but also validation, understanding and healing. They offer skills and coping mechanisms to use during this emotional life transition. The healing potential of this type of therapy may not be fully effective, however, if the patient is not concurrently engaged in his or her own inner soul work. An individual's desire to simply talk through certain events, although soothing, may also have the unintended effect of breathing new energy into the old story, allowing it to perpetuate and evolve indefinitely. Therefore, combining mental health therapy with other soul-focused and energetic modalities is highly recommended.

A Neuro-Linguistic Programming (NLP) practitioner can also be a good resource for dealing with anxiety, depression, communication issues, and even PTSD issues that may be related to the marriage and/or the divorce process. An NLP practitioner can assist an individual in understanding his or her thinking, behaviors, emotional states, and aspirations. NLP sessions are focused on the present, the here and now. Accordingly, they can help an individual move from the stagnation phase of divorce into a more positive phase — that of focusing on rebuilding the life they desire.

In 2008, I found myself struggling with circumstances surrounding my mother's passing; issues related to my father's passing long ago were also surfacing. In addition, I had just quit my employment with a law firm in order to open my own legal practice that focused on my holistic approach to divorce and was more in line with my beliefs and preferences. I was quite uncertain if my professional plan would be a success.

Fortunately, I met Dr. Mary Anderson, the founder of The Cardinal Center for Healing. At my time of need, synchronicity went into motion. Dr. Anderson's office was located above the law office I had just leased. She is a LCSW, an Intuitive, a Spiritual Counselor and a Psychotherapist — just the combination I needed.

Dr. Anderson developed what she refers to as Energetic Psychotherapy, a combination of modalities that bring together the body, mind, and spirit for deep healing. Her use of spiritual direction, intuitively guided talk therapy and bioenergetics provided me with a true holistic approach to healing. Dr. Anderson connected with and channeled my guides and loved ones in Spirit during each session. She initiated my efforts to call back the soul fragments I had scattered around and helped me understand the value of parenting my inner child.

Much of my deepest inner soul work was accomplished during and following intuitive readings from Dr. Anderson. She helped me deepen my ability to meditate, to channel, and to strengthen the connection with my main guide, Chala. She also assisted me in learning to trust the nudges from my soul to develop my mediumship, and to study Reiki, Shamanism, Transpersonal Hypnotherapy, Quantum Healing Hypnosis

Technique, (QHHT), Tarot, and other divination practices, all of which have been integral parts of my holistic approach to working with legal and mediation clients, as well as clients for spiritual life coaching.

I am sharing this information here, with my readers, as further evidence that when we sincerely seek guidance, the Divine Source over-delivers! Although we must do the work ourselves, the right people, the right tools, and the necessary resources, always show up.

## *Making Peace with Our Story*

We must make peace with our story, and acknowledge that it has served the purposes we intended for it, prior to our incarnation. We must deeply see the lessons, bless the experiences and the other souls who have contributed to our journey, recapture the fragmented pieces of our soul that we have abandoned along the way, and consciously re-integrate them into our story.

Once we are whole again, we can transmute and release the energy of the experiences that no longer play a role in our journey. At this point, we can bid a tender farewell to the former version of ourselves — the self we knew prior to pulling back the curtain on our life of illusion — and slowly awaken to our higher truth. From this place of empowerment, we discover that we have become our own guru! We can stop looking outside ourselves for the answers we seek. We can stop doubting ourselves and refuse to be captured by the spell of our perceived limitations. We can open the channel to Spirit from a place of inner power and belonging, rather than from a place of outer fear and weakness. We can lay down our belief in the cycles of karma, as though they are whips from a dark, mysterious place. We can acknowledge that karma may be released at any time, at the direction of our will.

However, none of this immense inner growth and fundamental change gives us a free pass to ignore the necessary work our soul intended.

There is a balance between eliminating past karmic cycles and manifesting the wisdom our soul intended by participating in these cycles. We do not have to remain trapped on the wheel of karma, but if we desire to turn it into a wheel of fortune or a new wheel of co-creation, we must be ready to take that transformative step. In *Messages from Masters, Tapping into the Power of Love,* Grand Central Publishing, Hachette Book Group (2000), Brian Weiss observes that "… karma is about learning, not about punishment." Acknowledging that grace can supersede karma, Weiss further states, "[g]race is divine intervention, a loving hand reaching down from the heavens to help us, to ease our burden and our suffering. Once we have learned the lesson, there is no need for further suffering, even if the karmic debt has not been fully repaid."

Ascension means that our consciousness has risen above the need to learn divine virtues in the same manner we have experienced for many lifetimes. It means we have evolved to the point that we embody these virtues, and have, therefore, blended fully with our higher self, as did the Ascended Masters before us. It also means that when the true gifts hidden within our DNA are ignited, we will use them — individually and collectively — only for the highest good.

We will never be free of the universal law of cause-and-effect; our choices will continue to have consequences. However, as our consciousness evolves, we will naturally make choices that are truly aligned with our soul, as opposed to aligned with the lower influences of our past experiences. We will witness the energetic chains losing their grip as we break free, one belief system or one pattern at a time, until we experience only our natural state of equilibrium. No more "should dos," "should haves," or "what ifs" — no time constraints, and no thoughts of failure or limitations — just absolute pure potential.

# 16

# The Soul's Anatomy / Light Body / Chakras

Most of us are familiar with what we perceive as our physical body, and how it functions. However, as we proceed through our daily lives, we sometimes forget that there is much more going on within and around us than what we can see with our naked eye — that is, more than the denser, slower-vibrating energy that makes up the physical body.

The human energetic system is vast and deserves a much deeper study than what can be discussed here. However, it is important to have a basic understanding of the symbiotic relationship of the energetic system and the role it plays in our human experience. A simple way to experience the feeling of energy is to rub your hands briskly together for ten seconds and then slowly move your hands apart. You will find that you can still feel the energy between your hands, and can even play with and mold that energy — as if you were handling a ball of clay.

The field of energy surrounding the body is commonly referred to as the light body, spiritual body, or aura. Also present, is our sacred chariot or Merkabah that extends beyond the auric field and contains the same geometric pattern of the universe. We are made up of the same electromagnetic properties as the energy field surrounding the earth. Living creatures, including trees, flowers, plants, and animals, are each surrounded by an energy field. Our aura, although invisible to the naked eye, is made up of several intermingling layers, and can extend many feet from the visible, physical body. The size and colors associated with an aura are unique to each individual, and fluctuate with our moods, thoughts, and experiences. Moreover, depending on where one is on his or her spiritual journey, an individual's aura may extend outward many feet.

On the other hand, an individual experiencing a loss, or another emotionally charged event, may have an aura that appears very condensed. Kirlian photography, invented in 1939 by Semyon Davidovitch Kirlian, is a process that captures the auric field of a living subject, as well as the colors present at the time the image is taken. Those with clairvoyant vision can see both the extent of an individual's aura, as well as the colors that are present when they are being perceived.

Most of us have picked up the "vibe" of an individual standing near us. Depending on our sensory impression, we either felt the desire to linger in the person's presence or to leave the space. Whatever the signal, at that time, we were tuning in to the person's aura. Animals too can sense energy; they know when danger is afoot, whether in the form of a human or an animal predator, a weather system, or another natural event such as an earthquake or an avalanche. Animals also respond to the positive emotions of love and joy. Similarly, as we learned from Dr. Masaru Emoto, water is also affected by energy. Dr. Emoto demonstrated that if water is exposed to loving and compassionate thoughts, the physical molecular make-up of the water is vastly different from water that is exposed to fearful or contradictory thoughts.

Each layer of our aura interacts with the physical body by way of energy points or chakras, which in turn direct vital life energy throughout the body in a network of pathways, currently referred to as the meridian system. Traditional Japanese, Chinese and Tibetan practitioners refer to these pathways as "channels" or "vessels." The Taiwanese culture calls these pathways "sen lines," and the ancient yogis who developed Ayurveda medicine referred to them as "nadis."

Most ancient cultures had some understanding that the internal organs of the body received their life force energy, or Qi, from one of twelve major meridian points. It is believed that when the correct balance of life force energy, or Qi, is achieved, any disease present in the auric field can be removed or healed prior to fully manifesting in the physical body. Many who have received acupuncture are familiar with the meridian charts displayed on the wall of most modern-day practitioners. It is becoming a more mainstream belief that the symbiotic relationship of our energy system plays an important role in our physical, mental, and emotional well-being.

With the advancement of ultrasound and magnetic resonance imaging (MRI) tools, what the ancients knew intuitively is becoming proven, as western medicine is now acknowledging these nonvisible aspects of our human makeup. The holistic approach to medicine is growing in popularity. Doctors often refer patients to alternate healing modalities, including Reiki and other forms of energy work. Many hospitals and cancer centers offer energy work as a regular part of their services and treatment programs.

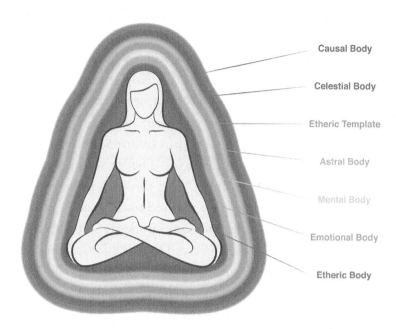

Causal Body

Celestial Body

Etheric Template

Astral Body

Mental Body

Emotional Body

Etheric Body

The health of our energy body plays a critical role in, and is a direct reflection of, how we experience our physical world.

## *The Light Body*

The layers making up the light body are not stagnant; they interpenetrate each other, as well as the physical body. Although several descriptions of the light body differ in terms of the labels attached to each layer, or perhaps the overall purpose of each layer, there is no dispute as to their existence. What follows is one understanding of the layers that make up the aura.

The first layer is known as the Etheric Body. The Etheric layer hovers close to the physical body and is connected to the physical body through the chakras and meridian system. This layer relates to the health of the physical body. Extending outward, the next layer is the known as the Emotional Body which is connected to the Sacral chakra. This layer represents our desires, emotions and feelings, and is known as the seat of human emotions. This layer is more fluid as it is in a constant stage of change depending on our mood.

The third layer is known as the Mental Body, which is connected to the Solar Plexus chakra. The Mental layer represents our thoughts, our cognitive processes, our belief system, and our general state of mind. This field expands and brightens depending on our mental activity. The fourth layer is known as the Astral Body, which is connected to the Heart chakra. The Astral layer reflects our relationships, and represents the energetic cords or attachments we have to others, and how they are formed. It is from this layer that we experience our intuition, conceptual thinking, and abstract ideas. The Astral layer is known as the window to our spiritual nature; it separates the first three layers which represent our physical nature.

The fifth layer is known as the Etheric Template, which is connected to the Throat chakra. The Etheric Template contains the blueprint of the physical body on the spiritual plane. This layer represents sound, vibration, creativity and communication. The sixth layer is known as the Celestial Body, which is connected to the Third Eye chakra. The Celestial layer reflects our subconscious mind; it is where our conscious mind connects to Spirit and unconditional love. Memories, our spiritual awareness, intuitive knowledge, integrity, and how we know we are connected to something greater than ourselves, rest within this layer.

The seventh layer is known as the Causal Body or Ketheric Template, which is connected to the Crown chakra.

The Ketheric Template vibrates at the highest frequency and represents our true self. We are one with the Divine Source at this layer. It stores all the wisdom, knowledge, experiences, talents and abilities the soul has gathered throughout time. It contains the blueprint of our spiritual path. The Akashic Records, or sacred book of the soul, is not separate from us; it is stored and accessed from within our own energy field.

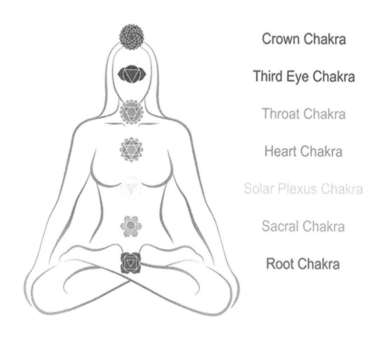

Crown Chakra

Third Eye Chakra

Throat Chakra

Heart Chakra

Solar Plexus Chakra

Sacral Chakra

Root Chakra

## *The Seven Main Chakras*

There are seven major energy points or chakras. The Sanskrit word, "chakra," means disk, or wheel, and refers to energy points in the subtle body. The concept of chakras and their functions can be found in many different cultures. The chakras are always in movement, and appear as wheel-like vortices of pure energy. The seven main chakras are located along the spinal column. When they are in balance, they align with the spinal column in a straight line. When one or more chakras are not in balance, their position may appear to spin to the right or left of their centers, or perhaps to the front or back of their centers. The chakras assist us in receiving, transmitting, and processing life energies, and each corresponds to a particular area of consciousness. They play an integral role in how the mind, body, and spirit operate as one holistic system. Each chakra is recognized as a focal point relating to our physical, emotional, mental, and spiritual energies. Each of the seven chakras, and the aspect of consciousness they serve, is briefly explained in the following paragraphs.

## *The Root Chakra*

The first chakra is known as the Root chakra, which is located at the base of the spine; it is associated with the color red, and the element of earth. On the color spectrum, red has the slowest vibration. This chakra forms the basis of our foundation, our sense of security. It deals with our survival instincts, our will to survive and our basic needs. It contributes to our self-awareness that we are human beings. The Root chakra controls the life force we receive from the earth, and is also the place from which our desires and imagination become manifest. When this chakra is balanced, we feel safe and supported — our perception of success and our placement in the world is neutral and stable, we feel content, and our roots are well-seeded and nourished. The chakras located above this energy point find their support from the anchor of a strong Root chakra and will likely experience fluctuations in their overall alignment if there is a weak foundation. When we feel the steadiness below our feet, we are able to work with the upper chakras with greater ease, and our ability to find clarity is enhanced.

When our Root chakra is out of balance or blocked, we may experience fear, anxiety, negativity, delusions, greed, and an overall feeling of instability and insecurity. We begin to lose our connection to the here and now, and we walk lightly rather than firmly on the ground. The lessons associated with the Root chakra concern our security in the material world, our stability, how we view and interpret our identity, our relationship with money, and how we characterize success. This chakra dictates our level of courage, our sense of balance, and our ability to offer patience and temperance to ourselves and others.

## *The Root Chakra during Divorce*

For those in the process of divorce, the Root chakra is the first affected. Although this will not apply to everyone, divorce naturally stimulates fear. Many will experience feelings of abandonment; they feel alone in the world, with no support. They feel as though their entire foundation is crumbling. Many lose their balance and become lost in a cycle of focusing too much of their attention on the past — and/or projecting negativity toward the future — rather than focusing their attention consciously. When we are grounded, we are focused on the here and now; therefore, if we can suspend our worries about the future and/or our failures in the past, we can more easily make decisions that are grounded in truth. For some, the thought of dividing marital assets can trigger strong survival instincts, regardless of the amount of wealth the family has accumulated during the marriage. For others, the idea of losing custody or having to share time with their minor children can trigger fear. For still others, the realization that they will need to receive or pay spousal support may trigger such fear.

For many, all issues present in the divorce process will serve as triggers. Once panic sets in, many have a hard time calming these emotions until the process is over, and accordingly, decisions are made from fear rather than from a place of clarity. It is important to be grounded from the beginning of the divorce and to maintain this grounding throughout the process.

## *The Sacral Chakra*

The second chakra is known as the Sacral chakra, located two to three inches below the navel. This chakra is associated with the color orange, and the element of water. This chakra governs our raw emotions and creativity as well as sexuality and reproduction. This chakra also controls the flow of emotions and thoughts. When this chakra is balanced, we are enthusiastic, passionate, and creative. We experience joy and self-respect, and are self-sufficient and resilient. Our relationships and ability to collaborate with others are in harmony. When this chakra is out of balance, we may experience inner conflict, issues with our sexuality, and an inability to express or process emotions. We might also experience jealousy, confusion, or begin a pattern of overindulgence. Addictions to food, sex, drugs, alcohol, and co-dependencies are birthed from an imbalanced Sacral chakra. The lessons associated with the Sacral chakra deal with our ability to give and to receive freely, and to learn the virtue of tolerance and appropriate surrender.

## The Sacral Chakra during Divorce

Those in the process of divorce who are experiencing an imbalance of the Sacral chakra may be unable to allow their emotions to flow naturally. They may become stuck in a particular emotion, or else be unable to feel at all. Despite how a party may have experienced the relationship with their spouse during the marriage, the end of the marriage can signal a loss of identity. In this state of mind, a party is unable to visualize a future after divorce, and consequently he or she may have trouble engaging in the free flow of proposed options during settlement discussions.

## The Solar Plexus Chakra

The third chakra is known as the Solar Plexus chakra, located between the navel and Sacral chakra, and is associated with the color yellow, and the element of fire. This chakra is the second emotional chakra and the seat of our knowingness, our power center; it is where intuition, or the "gut instinct," is formed and housed. Information or programs are received and transmitted from here, and we digest information and emotions from this chakra. The Solar Plexus chakra also governs our self-identity, our confidence and willpower. Our emotions are indicative of how aligned we are to our truth, who we really are and where our soul's journey is leading us.

When the Solar Plexus chakra is balanced, we have a healthy self-esteem, we are self-disciplined and confident in our choices and action. We exude radiance, warmth, and acceptance of others. A silver cord connecting the spirit body with the physical body is located within this chakra; when in balance, we experience a sense of immortality and know the truth of who we are. When this chakra is out of balance, we might experience overall dissatisfaction, anger, anxiety, depression, low self-esteem, procrastination, the inability to make decisions, the need to control or to exert power, and we might display uncontrolled emotional outbursts.

## *The Solar Plexus Chakra during Divorce*

Those in the process of divorce who are experiencing an imbalance of the Solar Plexus chakra may feel helpless, or show signs of irresponsibility. They might feel a loss of purpose and cannot visualize their future, or become hyper-focused on details and fail to see the big picture. Some might become overly fearful and even aggressive, demanding settlement terms that may not actually be in line with their integrity. People may become withdrawn, unable to identify their needs and might accept settlement terms not in their best interests. A party might feel the need to stall the process for as long as possible. When one's self-esteem is low and the connection to one's higher truth is jeopardized, a person remains unable to tap into their intuition, or knowing, of what is right for them. He or she may have no confidence in their decisions, and therefore have a hard time making a firm commitment.

Severe imbalance of the Solar Plexus chakra can create a tendency for a party to accept something they said they wanted, but then immediately change their mind. They may experience an uncontrollable need to exert power, without any concern for how it may affect them long-term. In addition, a party may be operating from an inner program they learned from their family, their culture, or religion, whereby they believe divorce is bad or sinful. As a result, they may not be self-confident throughout the process and may experience shame, distress, and feelings of unworthiness.

A party may be unable to process the amount of information they are given in a timely fashion. In addition to the legal information they must digest with each issue, a party must also respond to discovery requests, whether formal or informal, and be able to make sound decisions in terms of what they need; this is true whether they are in litigation or engaging in an alternative form of resolution. They also may have a hard time letting go of the marriage, and believe that their acquiescence to their spouse's demands of settlement will somehow change their spouse's desire to divorce.

## *The Heart Chakra*

The fourth chakra is known as the Heart chakra, located at the center of the chest. This chakra is associated with the color green, and the element of air. It operates as the bridge connecting the lower emotional chakras to the upper chakras. The first three chakras deal with the physical self; the Heart chakra deals with the spiritual self. It operates as an anchor to the life force that radiates from our higher-self to our lower-self. The Heart chakra is the seat of our healing, and our soul's destiny. It governs divine unconditional love, compassion, forgiveness, our generosity, and the ability to show respect and understanding to others.

When balanced, we feel harmonious with others, we tender love and care to ourselves and to others, we are content, at peace, and feel connected — we have an awareness of our oneness with all life. When the Heart chakra is out of balance, we may be suspicious or jealous of others, we may fear intimacy and feel disconnected. We may feel unworthy of love or unable to receive love. We might also have an overactive ego, which breeds selfishness.

## *The Heart Chakra during Divorce*

Those in the process of divorce experiencing an imbalanced Heart chakra may be detached from their higher truths. The seamless integration of their physical or earthly aspirations with their spiritual or higher aspirations is disconnected. Accordingly, they are unable to manage the challenge of divorce from a place of love, compassion, and appropriate discernment. They can become overly defensive and experience victimization, or they can feel the need to be a savior to their spouse, and fall victim to martyrdom. For these individuals, the ability to find peace through the act of forgiveness is blocked. Forgiveness is the key to successful settlement negotiations; it also produces the wings we need to fly, following a major life transition such as divorce.

## The Throat Chakra

The fifth chakra, known as the Throat chakra, is located in the center of the throat. This chakra is associated with the color blue, and the element of ether. The Throat chakra is the center of expression, communication, and creativity. It governs our ability to speak truthfully, both verbally and non-verbally; it is our source of self-expression. Our inspiration and ideas are processed and conveyed from this center. When balanced, we communicate clearly and authentically. We are considerate and speak with compassion, understanding, and honesty. We share our wisdom with another without fear of judgment. We are good listeners. When our heart and mind are aligned, we use our will appropriately and make decisions with skilled discernment and clarity.

When the Throat chakra is out of balance, we may be afraid to speak or express ourselves; or, we may speak without discernment or clarity. We may have an overactive ego that craves attention and needs to be heard. We may fail to listen, and therefore misinterpret the motives of others. We might misuse our wisdom and insight, and allow our uncalibrated ego to drive our will.

## The Throat Chakra during Divorce

Those in the process of divorce experiencing an imbalanced Throat chakra may be unable to express their truth. They may experience fear of speaking, and fail to speak up when something does not feel right to them. Alternatively, they may speak too much without a discerning filter, and fail to listen to others. They may be unable to tap into their higher wisdom, which will inhibit the natural flow between their connection to Spirit and their heart. The ability to be authentic and to speak clearly, the ability to use discernment and heightened listening skills, and the ability to see and hold a vision, are critical attributes to a successful negotiation process. An affirmation for the Throat chakra might be, "Within me is the courage to speak my truth in love — and my words will be received in love."

## The Third Eye Chakra

The sixth chakra, known as the Third Eye chakra, is located in the center of the forehead between the eyebrows. This chakra is associated with the color indigo, and the element of light. The Third Eye chakra is the center of insight or inner vision. It governs our inner knowing — our ability to understand higher truths so that we may have clarity of thought, sincere self-reflection, and self-responsibility. When this chakra is balanced, we are guided by our own intuitive wisdom and have peace of mind. We have a healthy imagination. Our inner vision extends far beyond what our physical eyes may perceive. When out of balance, we might experience cynicism, we may lack concentration, become judgmental, intolerant, and fail to show empathy for others. We may lose our common sense, and be unable to understand, or become disillusioned by, higher spiritual truths.

## The Third Eye Chakra during Divorce

Those in the process of divorce experiencing an imbalance of the Third Eye chakra may lack the ability to get past the physical distraction of the divorce, so they can tap into their inner sight, their inner knowing, their wisdom, and can sense the subtle shifts in energy. They may lack the ability to relax their mind enough to allow a shift in perception from their ego-mind to the mind of their soul. They may be unable to pick up the subtle signs that are there to move them towards a future vision and dissuade them from illusions.

## *The Crown Chakra*

The seventh chakra, known as the Crown chakra, is located at the crown of the head. This chakra is associated with the color violet, and the element of thought or will — or, as understood by some, emptiness. It is the Crown chakra that allows us to extend beyond our physical body and to experience the sacred oneness of all. It is where we experience enlightenment, and where our higher truths are downloaded. It is where we meet the divine self, divine will, and where we receive divine wisdom and inspiration. This is our direct line to Spirit. It is where we begin to understand the absence of duality, and the interconnectedness of all things.

When the Crown chakra is balanced, we feel a sense of deep peace, clarity, and joy. We understand the vastness of the universe, and our connection to the sea of all consciousness. We desire to serve selflessly, and to assist others in discovering their own truth from a place of brotherhood and unity. Our faith is strong and our ability to remain in the "now" is uncompromised. When this chakra is out of balance, we may lose our faith, experience anxiety, and perhaps denounce our own spiritual beliefs and knowing. We may feel a sense of superiority and separateness from others, and may lose our empathy for ourselves and others. We may also experience a lack of meaning or purpose in our life.

### *The Crown Chakra during Divorce*

Those in the divorce process experiencing an imbalanced Crown chakra may become disconnected psychically from their body and find it hard to physically engage in the divorce process at all. They may lose their connection to Spirit, and may miss the divine wisdom and inspiration that is being shared with them.

When our consciousness is balanced, we are in a state of equilibrium — our health improves, and our overall state of well-being is transformed. When our life energy is free to flow unobstructed, the circumstances in our life begin to flow with greater ease as well. Acknowledging and attending to the totality of who we are serves to accelerate the growth of our soul's journey, and brings us into greater alignment with our chosen path. We will always be guided by our inner compass, our intuition; however, when we are fully aligned, we are less likely to stray, to get lost or distracted. With full alignment, we have knowledge of, and are in harmony with, our purpose, our mission, our reason for being here. We are less clumsy with our ego, and can quickly assess and appreciate the circumstances in our life for what they are, as well as for what they are not.

We vibrate with a higher frequency and can begin co-creating the life we, as humans, would like to experience during our sojourn on the earth, while at the same time, remaining true to our soul's overall intention. Once mastered, we can then experience true abundance in all of its forms. We will experience the freedom we desire, the unbridled joy we crave, and will rest with peace in our heart.

With a greater understanding of how complicated, yet simple, our energy system is — and how it stimulates us to either thrive or decline — we can begin to consciously maintain a natural equilibrium. Setting aside a few minutes each day to check in with the totality of our being, and taking immediate action to correct any variations or blockages, is vital to our perception of reality and to our overall evolutionary process.

## *Aligning the Chakras*

There are many meditations and energetic processes that have been developed to assist us in the alignment of the chakra system. A simple Internet search will produce dozens of potential meditation options to choose from. There is no one-size-fits-all when it comes to processes intended to assist us in our healing efforts. We are each unique, and the way we respond is equally unique. Some individuals prefer guided meditations, and find it easier to follow the lead of the speaker. Some prefer a female voice while others prefer a more masculine tone. Some individuals prefer to meditate to soft music, without vocal prompts. It is helpful to try a few guided meditations until you find one that resonates with you. Still others prefer to sit, walk in nature, or lie down, all in complete silence.

It is important to stress that there is no set protocol for chakra alignment, nor is there a need to make it a complicated process. It is not necessary that we follow direction from a source outside of ourselves to accomplish this alignment. The best and most powerful process is one that is created from your own inner guidance.

In the beginning, it may be helpful to seek the assistance of a guided meditation or an energy healer to become familiar with feeling your own energy and understanding this new language. However, please trust that we all have the capacity to create a system tailored to us. I encourage you to sit calmly or lie down, with the intention of scanning the chakra system and balancing and clearing any blockages that may be present. The setting of this intention, coupled with simple visualization and relaxed breathing, is all you need to create an easy process that will work for you.

The following example is intended to provide you with a starting point from which you can develop your own chakra alignment process.

### *Designing your own Chakra Alignment Process*

*Begin with inhaling through your nostrils and exhaling through your mouth. As you inhale, consciously breathe in any negative thoughts and emotions you are experiencing — then, consciously expel and release these thoughts and emotions as you exhale. Be sure that you are exhaling longer than you inhale. Repeat this mindful breathing several times until you begin to feel settled. Focus your awareness on softening all the muscles in your body from the top of your head to the bottom of your feet.*

*Once you are completely relaxed, your heart rate has slowed down, you feel settled in your body, and your breathing has become soft and natural, begin with the Root chakra. Feel yourself anchored fully to the earth and work your way up to the Crown chakra. Whatever you sense as you focus your awareness on each chakra is right for you at that time. If the color of the chakra seems dull, focus on the color assigned to that chakra until the color intensifies and you feel a sense of fullness.*

*If the chakra feels off-center, visualize the chakra — however it may appear to you — spinning easily and freely, and realigning to its proper placement. You can also focus on the most positive attribute(s) of each chakra. There is no need to force any of this; a shift will happen naturally. If you feel a negative emotion, or if a negative thought begins to surface as you focus your awareness on a certain chakra, welcome the emotion or thought and thank it for its service to your journey. Then visualize the emotion freely flowing down to the center of the earth, to be transmuted into a higher emotion for the healing of all.*

*Once you have worked with each of the seven chakras, pay attention to how you feel, and spend a few moments in this space becoming familiar with how you feel when you are aligned and in harmony. Extend gratitude to your body for working with you, and to yourself for taking charge of your own well-being.*

The more you become familiar with how it feels to be in a balanced state, the easier it will be to know when you are out of balance. The more consciously aware you are of how you feel, the better you will be with knowing whether it is right for you to proceed with a certain action, or if you need to rebalance prior to going forward. The simpler the process, the more you allow your own inner healer to guide you. The more you become accustomed to working with your own energy, the quicker you can scan for imbalances and act in response.

Imagine how our interactions with others and our sense of well-being would shift if we each invested the time it takes to have a cup of coffee or tea each day to balance our own energy so that our mind, body and spirit are aligned and working collaboratively together. For those going through a divorce, this daily practice is so important. It is only when you feel aligned and your emotions are in a neutral space, that you should proceed with important matters concerning your divorce. The more you engage in this process, the easier and more natural it will become for you.

# 17

# Grief and Divorce / The Power of Forgiveness

## *Grief*

At times, individuals experiencing a divorce need to be reminded that a divorce triggers the same grief that we experience with the passing of a loved one. Divorce is the death of a marriage. It is the passing of a union between two people who have loved deeply and shared a life together, whether it was for a short period of time, or for most of their adult lives. The blending of the two souls that takes place during a marriage will naturally trigger a tremendous sense of loss when the people are separated. It is an interesting thought to ponder whether the loss we experience during a divorce is purely a human experience, or is rather the inner stirring of our higher knowing and connection with the soul we are separating from.

I have found that both parties experience grief at some point during the divorce, regardless of who initiated the divorce. Grief is universal and very personal to everyone. It is important, therefore, to know where you are in the grieving process as you proceed forward with your divorce. This acknowledgment is not intended for you to impress a judgment upon yourself. Rather, it is simply one factor in your holistic approach to caring for yourself during the divorce process. It is equally important to know, or to at least be sensitive to, where your spouse may be in the grieving process as well.

## *Five Stages of Grief*

One of the most popular theories on grief was given to us by Elisabeth Kubler-Ross, MD. In her classic book, *On Death and Dying*, Scribner, (1969), Kubler-Ross separated the grieving process into five distinct stages: Denial, Anger, Bargaining, Depression, and Acceptance. Although her work was originally developed for individuals who were terminally ill, the five stages have become a standard that is used to help us understand our responses to any loss in our life. Although additional stages have been presented by other authors over time, here we will focus on the five primary stages. Whether it is the loss of a loved one or a family pet who passed to the Spirit world, the loss of a relationship — the dissolution of marriage included — or the loss of any anchor we may have in our lives, these stages can be used to help us understand what we are experiencing, and to help us to move through the loss.

Over the years, Kubler-Ross expanded the breadth and depth of each stage of the grieving process, and in her book, co-authored by David Kessler, *On Grief & Grieving, Finding the Meaning of Grief Through the Five Stages of Loss*, Scribner, (2005/2014), she notes that, "The stages have evolved since their introduction.... They were never meant to help tuck messy emotions into neat packages.... They are responses to loss, but there is not a typical response to loss, as there is no typical loss.... They are tools to help us frame and identify what we may be feeling.... Not everyone goes through all of them or goes in a prescribed order.... Our grief is as individual as our lives...."

In a word on timing, Kubler-Ross and Kessler explained that "People often think of the stages as lasting weeks or months. They forget that the stages are responses to feelings that can last for minutes or hours, as we flip in and out of one and then another. We do not enter and leave each individual stage in a linear fashion. We may feel one, then another, and back again to the first one."

It is suggested that you consider reviewing the five stages of grief to better understand what you may be feeling during the divorce process, how you might move through these feelings, and to also understand where your spouse may be in the process. Having an awareness of where you and your spouse may be on the spectrum of emotions will help you navigate the divorce more productively.

If one party has accepted that the marriage is over and wants out of the union so strongly that he or she is ready to do anything to get there, but the other party is in denial that the marriage is irretrievably lost, or is experiencing another stage of grief, any attempt to negotiate an amicable settlement will be thwarted. Timing is an important aspect with most endeavors in life. With divorce, a little patience and compassion towards the party who may be in a different emotional space will ultimately serve to foster a more collaborative and successful negotiation process.

## *Denial*

When a divorcing party is surprised by their spouse's desire to end the marriage, or they simply did not pay attention to the signs of their own inner knowing, they may find themselves in a state of denial that will take some time to process. As the divorce moves forward, they may be unable to process and retain the information they will need to participate meaningfully in the divorce, and may find themselves stuck in disbelief that the marriage is over.

It is very common to hear statements from clients such as, he or she "will come to their senses; They are going through a mid-life crisis; They would never leave their children; They would never do this to me; They are just upset and overreacting right now; They will end this foolishness — stupidity — absurdity soon; They won't survive without me; I can't believe this is happening." Kubler-Ross and Kessler tell us that denial and shock help us to cope and make survival possible; that they are the psyche's protective mechanisms. They suggest that it can be emotionally overwhelming to fully believe the loss is occurring, while experiencing this stage.

If either party is experiencing this stage of grief, they will be unable to hear what they most need to hear from the professionals assisting in their divorce. They might be skeptical concerning communication with their spouse, or might even focus their attention on words that might mistakenly suggest to them a change of heart from their spouse. It is important to be sensitive to this emotional period if there is a desire to engage in a productive negotiation process in order to reach an amicable, enduring settlement. Showing compassion and, if possible, delaying the process until both parties are fully ready and present, will provide higher dividends in the overall process.

## *Anger*

When a divorcing party is experiencing anger, it is common that anger is worn as a mask for the deeper feelings of hurt and sadness that are being suppressed. It is important to allow anger to have a voice, whether it occurs in private moments of reflection, meditation, during conversations with a therapist, while taking a walk or while engaging in any activities that are needed to fully feel, acknowledge, and work through these feelings.

However, it is important to avoid expressing uncontrolled anger directly to your spouse, as that will only serve to hinder your divorce. A trained divorce coach might be a welcome resource to address this issue. When we allow our anger to have a voice, we can address the underlying emotions that we have infused into the anger and finally move forward. This expression of anger is unique to the situation, and to the individual. As the divorce proceeds, those participants experiencing anger may be feeling abandoned, may want to seek revenge against their spouse for wanting to leave them behind, or may be feeling anger towards themselves for not being able to "save their marriage."

Parties have incurred incredibly large amounts of attorney's fees during a divorce where anger was the predominant emotion fueling the process. Share your feelings with your attorney, and ask for his or her guidance. If your spouse is displaying anger, you might request that your attorney propose that a neutral divorce coach be retained to work with both of you, or you may benefit from retaining two coaches, so that discussions with each coach are private. Whatever it is that you and/or your spouse might be experiencing while in this stage — if you visit this stage at all — it is important to honor these feelings, and to allow the necessary time for the deeper feelings to be expressed, acknowledged, and perhaps forgiven — before proceeding with meaningful negotiations. When we are experiencing anger, we are not aligned with our higher self and so will not achieve the clarity necessary to make good decisions. If you are experiencing anger, it would be a great time to practice the exercise of aligning the chakras. You can, and will, get through this stage. We only experience anger when we have experienced love. Anger is a reminder that, at our core, we are love. It is love that mends our wounds, allows us to gift love to another, and reunites us with our highest expression.

## *Bargaining*

When a divorcing party is experiencing the bargaining stage, it is common to feel a loss of control and, therefore, extremely vulnerable. To regain control or some semblance of order, a few participants may feel the need to push their disorientation down the road by beginning to bargain with their spouse rather than negotiating terms of settlement. It is common that a party in this stage will make repeated requests to his or her spouse to seek counseling to save the marriage, or make statements such as, "I promise I will do whatever you want, if we can just stop this," and so on.

Sometimes, a party may use this stage to attempt to gain the upper hand over their spouse, depending on where that spouse is in the process. Kubler-Ross and Kessler noted that guilt is often "bargaining's companion." The "if onlys" cause us to find fault with ourselves and what we "think" we could have done differently. However, we know from our learning about soul contracts and agreements that, if it is time for us to move forward, we will be pushed, in one way or another.

It has been my experience that when parties choose to pause the divorce process and attempt reconciliation, it is, unfortunately, rarely successful. This is not, however, to suggest that every such attempt will be a failure. If the contract between the parties is not yet complete, or if the marriage is part of a higher contract with another individual, a temporary reconciliation may prove successful if the higher selves of both parties are able to communicate that they need additional time. For settlement purposes, it is only when a party is truly in his or her power, as opposed to handing this power over to their spouse in the form of emotional bargaining, that true participation in a meaningful negotiation process can occur.

## *Depression*

When those in divorce experience depression, they may feel extreme sadness, may withdraw from their family and friends, may appear to be shaken, may lose interest in whatever brought them joy at one time, and may even wonder what purpose their life has, outside of their marriage. Kubler-Ross and Kessler explain that when one is experiencing this type of depression it is not a sign of mental illness; in fact, it is the appropriate response to a great loss, a loss that cannot be fixed. It simply must be allowed to "be."

If your spouse or others encourage you to "just get over it," ignore the temptation to bury what you are feeling. This vulnerable state is the perfect time for you to initiate your inner soul work, make friends with the unaccustomed emotions, search deeper for their roots, and use this opportunity as a catalyst to further your soul's evolution. When we are feeling raw, naked, and exposed, we can crack open our protective shell and find the very place within us that will ultimately set us free. You may wish to speak to a therapist during this time; in fact, you should do so if you are having trouble managing this stage. Remember, however, that while the therapeutic work is meant to assist you in your self-discovery and in navigating the divorce process, it is not meant to replace your own personal inner soul work.

## *Acceptance*

When divorcing parties have reached the acceptance stage, they know that the marriage is over, and that a new reality awaits them. They may not be happy about the dissolution of their marriage, but they have resigned themselves to the fact that they must now look forward rather than backward. It is at this stage that honest and amicable negotiations can finally take place. When our sails start to point in the direction of where our ship is heading rather than where we have been, we are in a better position to properly align ourselves, gain the clarity we seek, and make healthy decisions. We begin to invest in our future, we can finally see our vision clearly, and a sense of excitement for where we are going begins to churn within us. When we allow this to occur, our soul provides the necessary wind we will need to reach the next phase of our soul's journey.

## *The Power of Forgiveness*

No book with a focus on divorce would be complete without a section dedicated to the power of forgiveness. The word *forgiveness* invokes several questions: What does it mean to forgive? What exactly are we forgiving? Who are we forgiving? How can we forgive when we are hurting and raw with emotion? When do we forgive? Must we speak the words, "I forgive you," directly to the one who hurt us? How will the act of forgiving assist us on our journey? How will the act of forgiving assist the other party on his or her journey? Do we even want to assist the other party on his or her journey? It may be that there are no issues in need of forgiveness — either for your spouse or yourself. This is of course, rarely true in a divorce, or with any meaningful relationship.

Forgiveness is the key to successful settlement negotiations; it also produces the wings we need in order to fly following a major life transition, such as a divorce. We must never forget that when someone hurts us, it is coming from their own woundedness. We are never asked to condone behavior that we perceive to be a transgression against us; we are simply asked to free ourselves from the energy associated with the behavior. The more we allow the natural flow of our emotions — by acknowledging the frustration, the anger, the disappointment, the resentment, the lessons we have learned from the experience, and then allowing them to alchemize or transmute into the empathetic, compassionate understanding of our soul — the more we free our soul from this dense energy and are able to again soar forward.

We also prevent the physical consequences of withholding forgiveness, which can lead to disease. Forgiveness is an act inspired by love. Our soul only operates from a place of love. When we step beyond the earthly field long enough to experience our soul's perspective on any event in our life, we allow our higher truth to guide us forward. It is important to note that a bruised ego is only temporary. Moving forward in a forgiving vibration of love is a gift we give to ourselves.

## *Forgiveness Ritual*

I encourage you to ask the questions proffered above, as well as those of your own. However, rather than pushing through the process and permitting your ego mind to respond in haste, allow the answers to rise up in you from your inner knowing — from that divine place within you that is directly connected to your higher self. Allow yourself to see the current situation from the lens of your soul's eyes; take a deeper dive into the lessons that are present.

Acknowledge the story (or stories) you have built around the experience(s), and then look further into the freshly shined, un-distorted mirror you have placed in front of you. Allow your inner voice to speak to you as you listen through the channels of the ears of your soul. Please do not turn away or hide from any emotions that may surface. Instead, feel into them. At this point, energetically invite your spouse into your space and visualize him or her sitting across from you. This visualization will assist you in the process.

Begin to build an energetic bridge between the two of you. Because you have been in the energy of your spouse throughout your marriage, you know their energetic

GRIEF AND DIVORCE / THE POWER OF FORGIVENESS

signature. Make the request that both your higher self and your spouse's higher self join in the discussion. Silently initiate a conversation about the contract existing between both of you. Affirm that it is your intention now to understand the contract and its lessons. This information is very important for you to understand prior to taking the next step on your journey.

Now, continue to go deeper. What was your spouse mirroring, teaching, and showing you by his or her behavior? Likewise, what were you trying to mirror, teach, and show your spouse by your behavior? What did the experiences highlight within you? This is an exercise that requires tremendous courage, a willingness to be exposed and vulnerable — both to yourself and to your spouse — and a level of compassion you have most likely never shown, either to yourself or to another human being. No matter the circumstance, there is always a higher lesson and greater understanding to be learned. Do not be afraid; wholeheartedly embrace each lesson. Your acknowledgement of every lesson carves new ridges and notches on the key to your own liberation.

Once you feel you understand the situation you are investigating, with intention and focused attention, acknowledge the aspect within you that was triggered by your spouse's behavior, and allow it to be fully integrated. Forgive yourself for missing opportunities to heal this wounded part within you sooner.

Visualize yourself wrapping the emotions and patterns of the lesson within a rainbow of beautifully colored balloons. Then release them in celebration, watching as they ascend out of your field of awareness. Imagine the balloons being alchemized into the most beautiful white light you can

203

envision. Bid Namaste fondly to that soul in human garb for this contribution to your soul's evolution.

If it feels right, send gratitude to your spouse for their role in this part of your awakening, and offer them your compassion-filled forgiveness. Notice their energy begin to shift. Yes, your forgiveness will indeed shift the energy of the very one who has harmed you. They, too, will now have an opportunity to learn, to grow and to expand their awareness. They will also be freed from the soul contract between you, forgiven for any transgressions or detours they may have taken from that contract, and hopefully, they will navigate their way forward on their own soul's journey. Many blessings are bestowed by this one loving gesture of forgiveness.

If this process does not cause you to see the situation differently, and to raise in you an honest desire to offer forgiveness to both your spouse and yourself, please do not fold your cards. Rather, continue to repeat the process until it opens your heart, and you know from the core of your being that you are deserving of acknowledgment, forgiveness, and most importantly, love, as is your spouse. As you forgive, you love, from that unconditional Divine Source within you. It is only our bruised ego that desires to hold on to the negative energy inherent in our "story." Our ego is fueled by our willingness to carry our story with us, and to breathe life into it — over and over. Truth becomes so distorted that the only way to learn the soul lesson is for us to unconsciously hit the repeat button — calling in a different experience each time, for the same lesson(s).

Forgiveness does not mean that we condone or bless the behavior, the action or inaction; it simply means that we release ourselves and the other person from the hurtfulness the behavior has caused, and instead, allow the higher spiritual lesson to shine through. The failure to forgive keeps the unhealed wound at the forefront of our energy field, instead of allowing it to heal. Rather than wear our wounds like a badge of honor, we must instead allow our hearts to wear the crown of compassion and thereby allow love to have the final word.

There are many resources available on forgiveness. However, it is important to remember that the most significant reason to offer forgiveness is to free yourself from the energetic cords of the contract between you and the person who has harmed, hurt and/or betrayed you — to transmute the cause and effect, the karma, the negative charge of that circumstance — and to forever negate the need to repeat the experience. If you will be co-parenting with your spouse, once you have completed the inner work and have removed the energetic cords joining you, take a moment to create a brand-new set of energetic cords — this time, made of soft, silk ribbons.

Doing this will allow you the freedom to control a flowing connection between you and your co-parent. During those times when you must work or communicate together, you can offer an energetic ribbon that you will loosely tie onto them for the purpose of a particular engagement. If you enjoy working with color, you may choose different colors for each set of circumstances. You may remove a ribbon following each encounter, or you may allow it to remain, knowing you can untie it and pull it back into your own energy at any time. This technique will also assist you with other challenging relationships in which a complete cutting of the energetic cords and the termination of further involvement is not an option.

Connie Domino, in her book, *The Law of Forgiveness, Tap into the Positive Power of Forgiveness and Attract Good Things in Your Life*, Penguin Group (2009), offers us the following affirmation that can be silently used to forgive another:

> *I forgive you completely and freely, I release you and let you go. So far as I'm concerned, the incident that happened between us is finished forever. I wish the best for you. I wish for your highest good. I hold you in the light. I am free and you are free, and all again is well between us. Peace be with you.*

Importantly, she offers us the following affirmation to forgive ourselves:

> *I forgive myself completely and freely. I release myself and I let me go. So far as I am concerned, the incident that happened between us is finished forever. I wish the best for me. I wish for myself my highest good. I hold myself in the light. I am free and all again is well with me. Peace be with me.*

Again, the act of forgiveness does not condone bad behavior, our own or another's. Forgiveness is a loving, selfish, selfless act which releases us from the dense energy keeping us shackled to the experience and to the person who hurt us. If we want to attract a different outcome going forward, and experience our life at our highest potential, we must first be willing to unlock the door to this higher frequency by using the key of forgiveness.

# 18

# A Dip into the Wisdom of the Tarot

A divorce is akin to pulling the archetypal Tower card from the Tarot deck. The Tarot consists of seventy-eight cards that are divided into sections, known as the major and minor arcana. The earliest deck of Tarot cards, known as the Visconti-Sforza, was illustrated by Bonifacio Bembo in Milan, Italy, in the fifteenth century. Although the cards were created as a royal court parlor game, over time the Tarot deck has evolved into what we recognize today — with the images symbolizing universal aspects or archetypes of the human experience. Archetypes are universal forms, primal patterns of thought inherent in and imprinted into the human subconscious.

The major arcana cards take us through the Fool's journey, an archetypical tale of human development. The word arcana means "secrets" or "what is hidden." Modern interpretations view each major arcana card as an allegorical representation of a certain archetype and phase of the human journey; they depict major life events, transitional periods, and larger life themes. The minor arcana cards depict the day-to-day events, feelings, and the people in our lives, as well the choices we make as we journey from one major life theme or phase to another. The images of the six major arcana cards that follow come from the modern Rider-Waite deck, illustrated by Pamela Colman Smith.

## *The Tower Card*

The Tower card is number sixteen of twenty-two cards on the Fool's journey. A brief look at the meaning of the Tower card, as well as the next few major arcana cards, may provide a perspective into the life transition that is inherent in divorce, and how we can evolve through it. There are many interpretations of the meaning of the images on each tarot card. The meanings shared here represent the author's interpretations, based upon years of working with

THE TOWER.

the tarot, as well as learning from many tarot scholars. Should you receive an instinctual feeling about an image, trust your own feelings, and use the experience as additional practice in learning how to listen to your own intuition.

The symbols on the Tower card present an image of a tower standing atop a rocky bluff against a gloomy, dark sky. The tower is in flames from a bolt of lightning, and images of both a male and a female are falling from the tower to the ground. It is through destruction and chaos that massive change and revolution are made possible. The Tower card symbolizes sudden, unforeseen change, upheaval, chaos, transition, loss, and the collapse of shaky foundations and old ideas. However, it also symbolizes liberation, higher knowing and an opportunity to build something better than what was previously standing. The energy and events surrounding the Tower card are meant to awaken us from our sleep and/or complacency and to encourage meaningful change.

The lightning bolt, viewed as a metaphor for divorce, pierces through our crown chakra and awakens us with a call to our own authenticity. The energy of the tower brings enlightenment — to bring light to what we are unable, or refuse, to see — to see through illusions and false belief systems, to notice the unstable foundations under our feet, and to be inspired to rebuild anew. Some individuals experiencing divorce cry out for their world to return to "normal." Others feel the force of the lightning as a call from their soul and have an inner knowing that a new and better "normal" is on the horizon, and that they are responsible for co-creating its design.

Divorce brings in chaos and change, and collapses our foundation. However, if we answer the call of the lightning bolt and use this pause in our journey as a stimulus to shine a light on our inner and outer worlds, we will be awakened to our truth. We must allow ourselves to see through our illusions and false beliefs. We must become aware of when and how we have surrendered our power, scattered fragments of our soul throughout our journey, and abandoned our inner child. We must also acknowledge how the influence of karma has governed our existence. Once done with all this, we can begin to take the steps to heal, to reunite with our higher self and to create a new life, a "new normal" — one that is aligned with our true essence and built upon a foundation of strength. Empowered liberation *can* be achieved during the process of divorce.

## *The Star Card*

The next major arcana card in the sequence of the Fool's journey is the Star card. The images on the Star card include a nude woman, representing vulnerability, humility, and a release of old patterns and limiting beliefs. She is resting, with one knee on the ground, representing her physical presence and connection to the earth, and one foot in a pool of water, representing her connection to the Divine Source, her inner world, and her intuition. She  is pouring water from two jugs — one into the pool of water, representing her subconscious and connection to the Divine Source, and the other onto the land. This water divides into five streams, representing her five senses, and depicts a natural flow between the two worlds of the conscious and subconscious.

The sun is shining above a rich, green, fertile land. Seven stars are clearly visible through a bright blue sky — representing the alignment of the seven main chakras. Following the destructive period of divorce, the energy of the Star card brings hope, faith, healing, creation, magic, connection, a time of peace, an understanding of the self and others, a fresh and broadened perspective, the desire to share information and resources with others, and renewed spirituality.

The large eight-pointed star depicted prominently at the top center of the card can be viewed as our own "north star." This card reveals that the subconscious has been stirred; it is up to us whether to follow the path forward or fall back into a slumber. The promise of hope is the first step — we are challenged to then take inspired action and develop practical solutions using the light of the stars as our guide.

If we answer the call to use divorce as a catalyst for our soul's evolution, we are met with renewed hope, balance, and the ability to commune with our higher self and Spirit more freely. We can take inspired actions as we move forward with a renewed faith that our "north star" will continue to illuminate the path ahead. We know that if we keep the fluidity between our higher self and our physical experience, we are in control; we are the only ones with the power to shine our light brightly or allow our light to dim. We control the calibration of our inner compass by our willingness to gift ourselves with the responsibility of self-care and self-mastery.

## *The Moon Card*

The next major arcana card in the sequence of the Fool's journey is the Moon card. Depicted on the Moon card in a night sky is a crescent moon within a full moon. Beneath the moon and between two pillars is a winding path leading to mountains in the distance. A dog and a wolf are shown howling at the moon, as a crayfish emerges from a pool of water. The moon represents a time of heightened intuition and inspiration, an evaluative and evolutionary cycle.

THE MOON.

The light of the moon is borrowed from the sun; its dim light provides a reflection rather than a clear vision. Thus, the Moon is an allegory for illusion — that things are not what they seem. The moon stimulates our imagination, our dreamscape, and shines a distorted light on those deep-seated fears and shadows within us. Accordingly, we are inspired to ask, "Are our fears an illusion? Are we being influenced by the thoughts of others, or are we governed by our own truth?"

The moon also represents deception and false information. The domestic dog represents those wild aspects of ourselves that we have tamed and settled. By contrast, the wolf represents the stirring of the wild beast within us — those aspects of ourselves we would rather ignore, but whose acknowledgment is necessary if we are to receive the light of the morning sun.

The crayfish is emerging from the sea of unconsciousness; although skeptical, it is ready to walk the path to the mountain of enlightenment to collect the blessings that await. The top of the mountain is where we align with the perspective of our higher self. The two pillars represent all forms of duality, the need for balance, and the birthing of something new. They provide a gateway, a portal of strength for us to travel through, where we become committed to defend our truth, shed our illusions, and reinforce our integrity. This is not an easy path, but worth the perseverance and courage needed to flow through the "up and downs" and "twists and turns" we will undoubtedly experience.

Unlike any other major arcana card, the Moon card depicts no human images. This is an internal journey; therefore, we are called upon to complete this inner journey ourselves. We are taken into the unknown, but we are also inspired to dream big and to use the divine tool of our imagination. We can seek assistance, but we must be willing to walk with our own soul as we proceed. As we brave the storm of uncertainty, on our search for neutrality and clarity, we can begin to conceptualize and develop the model of our future.

The rhythmic transformation of the moon each month is predictable. It controls the tides of the ocean, the ebb and flow of nature. The moon has a feminine energy. The masculine energy is tamed by the loving, accepting hand of the feminine. The intuitive, fertile, and compassionate nature of the feminine energy within each of us, is needed to fully birth an evolved consciousness.

As we walk through the energy of the Moon card in divorce, we are encouraged to go deeper, and to take the hand of our higher self and request to be shown our truth beyond the illusions. We must discover where we have been deceived, and, more importantly, how we have been deceiving ourselves. What mysteries can be uncovered concerning the soulful relationship with our spouse, so that the human transition of divorce can be resolved from a place of truth, integrity, and divine love? What must be allowed to come to the surface to be addressed, acknowledged, loved, transformed, and released — if we are to welcome in the warmth, fertility, and light of the sun? When we seek assistance on our journey of enlightenment and follow the guidance, we will find ourselves standing proudly on the mountain top, aligned, and blended with the two worlds. Indeed, a commitment of courage is necessary to jump into the depths of the unknown; however, after experiencing the loving guidance of our higher selves and our devoted guides, we will wonder what took us so long to make this move.

## *The Sun Card*

The next major arcana card in the sequence of the Fool's journey is the Sun card. Beneath a prominent large sun in a blue sky, a cheerful infant is riding on the back of a white horse. He is emerging forward from a tended inner garden where sunflowers are blooming. The sun brings knowledge, enlightenment, clarity and further illuminates his path. The sun breaks through the darkness of both our inner and outer worlds and brings in a time of good

THE SUN.

fortune, happiness, and joyfulness. The inner child has been freed, and his soul is finally allowed to shine through. His chains and burdens have been lifted. His illusions and fears have been alchemized. The power and adrenaline of the horse will provide the stamina needed to accomplish the next phase of the journey. We can, finally, see the world as joyful and united.

The sun also represents power. The Sun card shows us that we are on the right path, and that positive outcomes will be birthed from our courageous efforts. The sun is necessary for life to exist and to thrive. However, the sun can also burn and destroy. The sun is a constant; all living things are treated equally under the rays of the sun. As we evolve, we must be diligent in our efforts to balance the open excitement and immaturity of the child with the wisdom gained from our past experiences. The face of the sunflower always follows the light of the sun. With unwavering faith, we too must make decisions from a place of clarity and truth — which only a focus influenced directly by the radiance of the sunlight can bring.

As we journey through the Sun card in divorce, we are well on our way to creating a life that is good for the soul. We have done much of the inner work asked of us. We are enlightened, we feel whole and lighter from the release of what no longer serves us. We can see the path in front of us, and are ready to forge ahead into the new life that awaits. We have the fearless giddiness of our inner child blended with us. We can feel the stability and firmness of the new foundation we are creating, as we continue to walk forward, one step at a time. With our eyes and focus on the light, the *jewels of wisdom* gained from our journey will become our most precious cargo.

## The Judgement Card

The Fool will have some traveling to do through the energy of the Judgement card before moving into the final major arcana card. The images on the Judgement card include an angel (Archangel Gabriel) blowing a trumpet with a white flag with a red cross attached. Naked men, women and children are seen emerging from wooden caskets with their arms extended outward. This card symbolizes a call for a final shedding of the old ways of living, the old ways of  thinking, the breaking free from conditioning — the death of the former self, and the rebirth of the new, integrated, awakened self. We are ready for judgment; however, in this instance, we are reminded that "we" are our own judge. It is important that we judge ourselves and each other with compassion and a belief in redemption, rather than fearing punishment. The upward movement of the sleeping serpent, the Kundalini, rising and awakening within us, will bring in moments of intensity that may cause us to recoil. In this final stage of self-reflection, we are asked again if we are living from our truth. Are we making choices that serve our highest good, and the highest good of all involved? Are our past experiences still influencing our fate, or have we integrated our inner growth with our outer choices? Are we stumbling into delusional thinking, or have we integrated our intuition with our intellect? Has the ego been allowed to insinuate superiority and a return to hierarchical thinking?

The judgment phase is a realization that a shift has occurred within us, but whether we have fully embodied this shift will be the essential analysis. Slight adjustments and tough choices may be necessary if we are to harvest the fruits of our efforts. We must visit this time with humility and integrity if we are to avoid a one-step-forward, two-steps-backward scenario. Compassionate action towards ourselves and others, coupled with the blending of our soul and our intellectual reasoning, must become the new template.

As we move into the phase of the Judgement card, whether during or after the divorce, we are reminded that the journey to enlightenment is an ongoing commitment, and that our soul is always evolving. We are asked to humbly review our progress. Are there areas in our life we have refused to visit? Are we still holding on to things and people no longer serving our highest good? Are we still carrying loss, pain, rejection, or anger within us? Have we truly forgiven ourselves? Have we truly forgiven our spouse? Are there others in line waiting to be forgiven? Have we slipped into old patterns and just need a gentle reminder?

It is important that we remain observant and diligent in our efforts. When we fall out of alignment, we must simply take the necessary actions, forgive ourselves, and jump right back on the path. Making it to this point must be celebrated. Over time, we begin to bring humor into our experience and even find ourselves laughing at our faux pas. We will slip now and then, but after all the hard work we have done, our recognition and response time will be much quicker.

## *The World Card*

The final major arcana card of the Fool's journey is the World card. The images on the World card depict a naked woman dancing and hovering over the earth, holding the batons of the Magician in each hand. She is balanced, content, and has achieved success in her journey to enlightenment. She has reached the highest point on the Wheel of Fortune. Like the cosmic dance of Shiva, the World card dancer has one foot pointed downward, symbolizing a connection  to the earth, while the other foot is raised, symbolizing the freedom of the soul. She is dancing in the middle of a green wreath, symbolizing a healed spirit, the acknowledgment of the benevolent love of the Divine Source, endless potential, and the simultaneous connection to all things — and yet to nothing. She is recognizing her place as a cosmic citizen. Red infinity symbols are tied to the top and bottom of the wreath, symbolizing the infinite nature of the universe, the connection between the spiritual and physical worlds, and the fact that we are residing and dancing in both worlds at once. The sky is blue, and the sun is providing the light needed to celebrate the end of a long journey. In each corner of the World card there is a figure of a lion, a bull, a cherub, and an eagle. Together, they symbolize the cyclical nature of life, the four elements of the earth and the fixed signs of the zodiac. They are reminders of the constant need to strive for balance as we proceed forward. The fifth element of space is depicted in the blankness surrounding the human figure, symbolizing a sea of unlimited potential. With a peaceful heart, it is time to enjoy the fruits of our labor. We have made much process on our healing mission — we have created the space for our highest idealizations of utopia to become a reality on earth. We have the tools we need to begin the walk of the Fool's journey into the next stage of our evolutionary climb.

When we reach the phase of the World card in our divorce, we have reached a place of complete harmony. We have created the space for newness to flood in, and for our highest expression to be materialized. The universe begins accelerating the response to our inner needs and desires by bringing synchronistic events, people, and resources into our lives. It is a time for celebration, a time to be joyful, and to embrace this amazing accomplishment. We are to be congratulated for a job well done!

Our soul is ready to take us, in the shoes of the Fool, on our next adventure. As our journey continues, we know that we have *collected the jewels from the events of our past* and that the energy from these events has been fully alchemized from a source of pain and confusion into a source of divine love and wisdom. We have gained the skills we need to navigate any experience from a place of neutrality, and alignment with our higher self. With a fresh perspective, we are beginning to see our future vision emerge.

# 19

# Envisioning Your Future

In addition to the inner healing journeys relating to past events and circumstances, it is equally important to focus your energy on what is in front of you — as soon as possible. In fact, the focus of the inner work will assist you in the creation of your future vision. Regardless of which party decided to initiate the divorce, or if the decision to dissolve the marriage was made jointly, *it is imperative that you recognize this time as a ripe opportunity.* If you are willing, and have invested quality time in your inner work, you are in the best position to co-create your future, rather than surrendering to, and allowing your future to be shaped by, the divorce process.

Spending time contemplating how you would like to see your life evolve following the divorce will help shift your energy away from any stagnation that may be present, and from clinging to past beliefs and paradigms of what you thought your life would be, or should be. This shift will reunite you with your faith, with the light and curious nature of your inner child, and with your soul's larger plan or theme for the next phase of your journey.

The following is a list of recommended questions to be considered:

- What do I want my life to look like when this transition is over?
- Have I been living "my" life, or have I been living someone else's life?
- How do I personally define happiness or joy?
- When was the last time I felt happy or joyful?
- What brings me the most joy?
- What do I know my soul's gifts to be?
- How have I been expressing these gifts?
- How would I like to express these gifts in the future?
- What is truly important to me?
- What do I want to spend my time doing?
- What gifts have come from past experiences that I might have defined as challenging at the time they were occurring?
- How might these gifts assist me now?
- What is one important thing about me that I have set aside?
- What does my inner child want me to know?
- What is it that I really want?
- What do I need to feel safe?
- What do I want my home environment to look like?
- What do I want my home environment to feel like?

- Who do I want to be present in my life?
- Who are the people in my life who are no longer feeding my soul?
- Am I fulfilled in my current profession?
- What am I most interested in now?
- What do I want to learn more about?
- What do I know that I can share with others?
- Have I explored what my higher purpose or mission might be?
- Am I living my purpose, or moving towards it?
- What do my higher self and Spirit want me to know right now?

You might choose to pose several of these questions in one sitting, or you might choose to consider one or two at a time in successive sittings. Have faith, and know that the answers are available to you. There are no "I don't know" responses when you are coming forward with integrity, and from a place of true alignment. Your soul will always guide you to the answers that will serve your higher purpose. You might even choose to set some of the questions aside until your divorce is finalized; however, to capture a vision that truly reflects YOU, and one that is co-created with your soul, it is helpful if you allow yourself to fully engage.

We are all here to learn different aspects of love, forgiveness, compassion, patience, understanding, integrity, peace, and yes, joy! The world around us reflects the world within us. As we heal and polish our inner world, so too does our outer world begin to shift and shine. The transition of divorce provides a prime opportunity to begin designing and envisioning a future that reflects who you are now, what is important to you now, and one that will bring joy into your present experience.

## *Focused Meditation to Create your Vision*

Start by slowly inhaling to the count of four, then exhale to the count of four, and repeat this process four times. This simple breathing technique will bring you to your heart-space and will shift your frequency. With each exhalation, scan your body from the top of your head to the bottom of your feet. Imagine that your muscles are softening as you make your way down your body. Notice that all tension present in the body is being collected and released into the earth from the soles of your feet, to be transmuted into healing energy for all. Remember, the simpler the process, the more likely your ego mind will surrender and allow your subconscious mind to assist you. As you continue to breathe naturally, shift your awareness to the base of your spine. Imagine a cord extending from the base of your spine down into the earth. Notice the energy pulling and grounding your foundation until you feel comfortably solid in your space. Now wrap this cord around a large crystal, with the intention that it holds you securely in place. Envision that, from this crystal, there is a stream of nurturing energy from the earth traveling up through the cord. Beginning with your Root chakra, as the energy moves up through each chakra, breathe into that chakra the intention of balancing, and imagine each chakra spinning free of any blockages. If you are inclined, you can even imagine the color of each chakra becoming brighter as you set your intention.

Once you have completed the process in your Heart chakra, bring your awareness directly to your Crown chakra. Imagine a beautiful bright white light streaming downward toward you from the Divine Source. Allow this bright light to cascade all around you and to enter your Crown chakra. Breathe into your Crown chakra the intention of balancing and purifying. Imagine the Crown chakra spinning free of any blockages. Bring in the chakra color, if you are so inclined. As the light continues to descend, repeat this process with the Third Eye chakra and then the Throat chakra. Now imagine the light descending further and joining the earth's supportive energy in your Heart chakra. Allow this merged energy to permeate your entire body and visualize the energy flowing continuously in and out of your physical body several times in a continuous flow as though you are cycling or creating a fountain of light around you.

*If you are experienced in your meditation practice, you may have an induction that brings alignment and allows you to feel your power rising within a few moments. Please feel free to adjust this induction to best suit your needs.*

Imagine you are surrounded by a pyramid of bright light from the Divine Source. This pyramid will serve as your protective shield while you journey. Once you feel grounded, your chakras are balanced and spinning freely, and you feel that the bridge between your heart and higher self is connected, take a deep breath. With a strong exhale, intend for, and feel your energy expanding beyond your physical body until you feel as though you are simply floating. Spend a few moments floating in this quantum field, where everything is known, and anything is *possible.*

As you sit in this field of possibility, allow yourself to simply daydream, to imagine, and allow your thoughts to flow freely without judgment. If negative thoughts of your current situation intrude, visualize them as clouds simply floating past you. When your mind settles, ask yourself the questions you have chosen from the recommended list or even a few of your own. You will be guided as to how much time you will need with each question you have posed. Each time you sit in this meditation, the easier it will be for you to shift your awareness from the current situation to your field of creation. Write down the answers you receive after each meditation session. Give yourself time to contemplate what you have learned. Some answers may surprise you. The more you are engaged, the sooner you will begin to see the design of your future begin to unfold and take shape.

Once you are comfortable with your vision, it is time to work with it. By using the meditation induction above, or one of your own, sit with a clear intention, and with focused attention begin to visualize and play out your vision. Stay focused and aligned. Invite this vision in. Step into each scene as it plays out in your inner mind. Hold the vision. Feel it as though it is happening right now. Notice how your body feels as you are living your future design. Hold on to these emotions for as long as you can. An energetic template is created as soon as the thoughts are formed.

You are operating as the magician of your own life! Breathe into the knowing that you are the creator, and that you are deserving of the life you envision — believe. Sit with your vision daily and allow your body the experience of living in this timeline, as though it is happening right now — until it becomes rooted within your cellular structure. The more you can focus on this vision and hold its frequency, the more you are calling it towards you. Whenever you are faced with moments of doubt, simply repeat the process. You will find that you are able to hold the vibration of your vision longer and longer, until it becomes second nature to you. Before long, just the thought of your vision will create a shift in your consciousness and will stimulate your body's reaction. With each sitting, you are strengthening your connection to your own inner wisdom, your higher self and to Spirit; and you are strengthening your faith in knowing that anything is possible, that all will be well, that all is well.

During these focused meditation sessions, you are expanding your energy field. At the end of each session, focus on pulling your energy back to you. Some may feel the space around the physical body decreasing as the energy is consciously drawn back in. Stop as soon as you feel you are comfortable and in your normal state. There is no need to worry if you do not feel a sensation; just set the intention to bring your energy back to you and know the process will be completed.

As you gift yourself permission to accept and honor your worthiness, you are simultaneously raising your frequency. Give gratitude for all the experiences that have brought you to this point and for the synchronicities that will occur in the realization of your vision. When we sit in gratitude, our frequency rises exponentially. Recalling any event in our life, big or small, when we felt tremendous gratitude towards someone, or a certain event, will shift our energy and raise our frequency. If at any time you begin to experience self-doubt, worry, anxiety, or you hear the voice of your nagging saboteur questioning how your vision will be accomplished, pause: you are out of alignment. Take a deep breath through your nose and exhale longer than you inhaled. Repeat this several times until you can feel your heartbeat slow down. This will bring you into the present moment. Let any thoughts that come up float by you as though they are clouds.

When your heartbeat slows down, the muscles in your body begin to relax, and your breathing becomes steady and calm, silently ask yourself, "What is it that I am really feeling anxious about? Is my anxiety or worry attached to what is happening right now, or is it rooted elsewhere in my journey?" Set the intention to visit your Akashic Records, and state that you are ready to receive this information now.

Keep breathing into your questions. Allow yourself to use all your senses to fully explore what is surfacing — even if in a different time, a different place, or perhaps a different lifetime. Allow yourself to be open to all *possibilities* that may surface with a sense of wonderment and curiosity. When you feel you have uncovered the root of the emotion, take a deep breath, and allow yourself to view the event as a loving observer would. Allow this wounded part of you an opportunity to be acknowledged, to speak to you, and to share with you why it remains in your energy field. What blessings or lessons are there for you to uncover? Once you feel comfortable with the answers you have been given, send love and gratitude for the blessing or learning experience, and visualize the event and the emotion fully integrated, transmuted, and released from your energy field. This event no longer serves a higher purpose, and will no longer influence you and your decision-making process.

# 20

# Preparing for Negotiation and Settlement Conference

*"... Out Beyond Ideas of Wrongdoing and Rightdoing,
There is a Field.*

*I'll Meet You There ..."*

*Rumi*

O nce you have an understanding of the law in your jurisdiction as it pertains to the facts of your case, you are comfortably informed about the assets and liabilities and other matters associated with your divorce, you have made a good-faith effort to engage in the inner work and forgiveness ritual that has been suggested, and, you have awakened a vision of the future you wish to experience, it is time to go behind the scenes and prepare the field for your negotiations and settlement conferences.

As Albert Einstein advised, "We cannot solve our problems with the same level of thinking that created them."

Thus, to fully prepare for a successful negotiation, your perspective must be expanded. All labels of good and bad, right and wrong, fair and unfair, just and unjust, must be jettisoned. Any expectation of a particular outcome, other than to intend a result that will be in the highest interest for you and for all involved, must be surrendered. Continue to hold your vision as your focus.

Try to avoid any attachment to a particular provision of your settlement agreement. Completely step out of the paradigms you have been accustomed to, and allow your intuition to guide you. Just as Rumi suggested, "Out beyond ideas of wrongdoing and rightdoing, there is a field. I'll meet you there..." You will first visit this field, and from there, you will create the space from which to participate in the settlement process.

Whether or not you are preparing for trial, a settlement conference, or a settlement discussion just between you and your spouse, the space you will create in this exercise will work for each circumstance. Please read through the process more than once, prior to starting. You will want to become familiar enough with the steps so that you can proceed without the need to break your concentration in order to re-read a section.

If you feel the process is too cumbersome, feel free to delete any steps that do not resonate with you, or that you do not find helpful. You may need to repeat this exercise more than once to feel fully prepared. *Except for the inner healing work, the time invested in this exercise is more important than any other preparation you will undertake.* Preparing the field and aligning your energy in advance will not only attune you to your highest potential, but will also ensure that your energy will be the dominant influence during the negotiation process.

## *Focused Meditation to Prepare the Field*

The induction phase of this meditation mirrors the induction section of the Focused Meditation to Create your Vision.

Start by slowly inhaling to the count of four, then exhale to the count of four, and repeat this process four times. This simple breathing technique will bring you to your heart-space and will shift your frequency. With each exhalation, scan your body from the top of your head to the bottom of your feet. Imagine that your muscles are softening as you make your way down your body. Notice that all tension present in the body is being collected and released into the earth from the soles of your feet, to be transmuted into healing energy for all. Remember, the simpler the process, the more likely your ego mind will surrender and allow your subconscious mind to assist you. As you continue to breathe naturally, shift your awareness to the base of your spine. Imagine a cord extending from the base of your spine down into the earth. Notice the energy pulling and grounding your foundation, until you feel comfortably solid in your space. Now wrap this cord around a large crystal, with the intention that it holds you securely in place. Now envision that, from this crystal, there is a stream of nurturing energy from the earth traveling up through the cord. Beginning with your Root chakra, as the energy moves up through each chakra, breathe into that chakra the intention of balancing, and imagine each chakra spinning free of any blockages. If you are so inclined, you can even imagine the color of each chakra becoming brighter as you set your intention.

Once you have completed the process in your Heart chakra, bring your awareness directly to your Crown chakra. Imagine a beautiful bright white light streaming downward toward you from the divine source. Allow this bright light to cascade all around you and to enter your Crown chakra. Breathe into your Crown chakra the intention of balancing and purifying. Imagine the Crown chakra spinning free of any blockages. Bring in the chakra color if you are so inclined. As the light continues to descend, repeat this process with the Third Eye chakra and then the Throat chakra. Now imagine the light descending further and joining the earth's supportive energy in your Heart chakra. Allow this merged energy to permeate your entire body and visualize the energy flowing continuously in and out of your physical body several times in a continuous flow as though you are cycling or creating a fountain of light around you.

*If you are experienced in your meditation practice, you may have an induction which brings alignment and allows you to feel your power rising within a few moments. Please feel free to adjust this induction to best suit your needs.*

Imagine you are surrounded by a pyramid of bright light from the Divine Source. This pyramid will serve as your protective shield while you journey. Once you feel grounded, your chakras are balanced and spinning freely, and you feel that the bridge between your heart and higher self is connected, take a deep breath. With a strong exhale, intend and feel your energy expanding beyond your physical body until you feel as though you are simply floating. Spend a few moments floating in this quantum field where everything is known, and anything is *possible*.

When you are ready, using your imagination, visualize yourself in a conference room in which you are seated at one end of a table. Imagine your spouse is seated at the other end of the table, facing you. This table is made of pure white crystal with a smooth surface. It will serve as a physical representation of the quantum field, and holds within its vibration all the knowledge of the universe, and specifically, the past, present and future soul connections between you and your spouse. Imagine that the room is full of floor-to-ceiling windows with an open atrium above allowing light waves of many colors to flood the room. You may imagine this room to be sparsely furnished or fully furnished, so long as it is filled with a décor that suits your taste.

You notice that the color on the wall is soothing, and invites creativity to flow with ease. Notice how it feels to be securely seated in your chair and supported by the earth beneath you. Acknowledge that there are others seated in the chairs around the table. Regardless, visualize these participants as devoid of any distinct facial features and wearing plain white clothing. These other participants might include the attorneys in your case; however, they will certainly include your guide(s) and your spouse's guide(s), who will be assisting you. Do not worry if you have trouble visualizing; just trust yourself.

Take a few moments to greet the other participants in the room, and then focus your attention on your spouse. In these few moments, you are preparing an intuitive space that replicates your pre-incarnation planning sessions with your spouse as closely as possible. Acknowledge your spouse with the Namaste greeting, and begin to see him or her outside of a human costume. Allow him or her to reveal themselves to you from the perspective of their soul, absent earthly burdens, imperfections, judgments, and other attributes that may cloud your vision. Intend that the neutrality that was present when you and your spouse designed your earthly partnership is present again, and available to you now. Let your spouse know that you see him or her, at a soul level — eye-to-eye, heart-to-heart, soul-to-soul.

Build an energetic bridge between your heart and theirs, with the intention that this bridge will facilitate an environment of safety, neutrality, and integrity. Intend that you will be allowed to speak and to make decisions from a place of integrity, regardless of how these decisions may be received by those outside this connection. Also, set the intention that you will only receive communication and honor decisions from your spouse that come from the seat of his or her own integrity.

Now, from this place, begin to freely speak to your spouse about what you have envisioned for your future, and what you need in order to gracefully move forward. Share what is important to you. Be specific, and share the reason why something is important to you. What is the *interest* behind your desire? If you have children, express your ideal co-parenting relationship and what you envision as a healthy parenting / custodial schedule that will meet the best interests of your children, as well as the needs of the two of you. If there are certain assets of the marriage that are important to you, share this with your spouse. Include what these assets mean to you and what your underlying *interest* in them is.

In this conversation, do not hold anything back. This is a safe place for you to plant the seeds of cooperation and understanding. If you feel you need financial support, share this with your spouse. Discuss not only why it is important that you have the security you need to move forward financially, but that you also understand that he or she, too, must have sufficient resources for their individual journey forward. Whatever it is that you desire, from the broadest perspective down to a certain silver fork or spoon, share these thoughts freely with your spouse.

Spend a few minutes sharing the details of the desired future you have been envisioning. Share this vision absent any concern about how the divorce process may help you manifest it; just speak with sincerity and joy about what you envision. You may even include any thoughts you may have for your spouse. As you communicate certain concepts and desires, send love to your spouse — not romantic love, just pure, unconditional, divine love. Infuse your words with love as you send them across the table. As you speak, imagine your spouse listening to you from a place of love, through the channels of the ears of their soul, from a place outside of linear time and without human safeguards. Imagine his or her positive and loving reaction to the information you are sharing. Imagine your spouse holding the perspective of his or her higher self, where anything and everything is *possible* — that he or she is wanting you to have peace, safety, joy, and contentment — and realize that your spouse shares the same desires for him or herself.

Envision your spouse understanding that we are all connected, and that whatever affects you, be it good or bad, will have an impact on him or her as well. Now see the two of you drafting amendments to your soul contract which will achieve these higher goals, you do not have to know what the amendments include. If either of you wish to terminate the contract altogether, and there are no children of the marriage, allow your higher self and your guides to assist you in this regard. See your spouse responding to you as a comrade — instead of an adversary — on your team, as a member of your soul family in Spirit.

Now breathe into this vision, notice how it feels to have a successful discussion, to be heard and respected, to design a settlement embracing and reflecting your highest good and deepest interests — even if you are unaware of the details of the settlement. Appreciate the knowledge that, when you operate from a place of integrity and allow your spouse the safety to do the same, miracles are possible. Sit in this energy for as long as you need to. Do briefly check in with the others who have been at the table with you through this journey, and ask for any feedback. However, know that you have both been guided and supported during this process.

Your guides, along with the Divine Source, have already started the process of creating synchronicities that will support your vision and help you bring it into manifestation. Your only commitment is to remember the vision, stay out of doubt, and maintain the frequency that you experienced during this exercise. Make that commitment now. Seal this experience within the energy of the Namaste greeting. That is, intend for the Namaste greeting to hold the energetic signature of the "field" you have created, as well as the conceptual resolutions you have shared.

During this focused meditation, you expanded your energy field. At the end of your meditation session, focus on pulling your energy back to you. You might feel the space around your physical body decreasing as the energy is consciously drawn back in. Stop as soon as you feel you are comfortable and in your normal state. There is no need to worry if you do not feel a sensation, just set the intention to bring your energy back to you and know it will be completed.

Repeat this process prior to each formal settlement conference, private settlement discussions with your spouse, and before trial, if applicable. Remember, you are preparing the field for these future experiences. You are pre-setting the atmosphere and the energy that will control these events. You are infusing neutrality and integrity into the energy, along with your conceptual ideas for resolution. You are not placing attachment on any particular outcome. You are holding the vibration of your future vision and have faith that your needs will be met — and perhaps exceeded. If we place attachment on a particular outcome, we might miss the opportunity of a resolution that will exceed our expectations. Conceptual ideas of resolution, rather than specifics, will help you see the bigger picture during any discussion.

## The Namaste Greeting

The Sanskrit word, "Namaste" is a reminder that we must not forget that we are all souls, and that the divine light resides within each of us. As we greet another with a Namaste bow, or simply state, "Namaste," to another, we are acknowledging their soul, the divine presence in the other. Notice this gesture bypasses the illusion of the physical body and other human characteristics of the one greeted and travels directly to the divine nature. It strips through the ego and apparent limitations and, in that one moment, acknowledges that we are all the same, we are equal, we are whole, we are love, and that we can see ourselves in another.

When we are preparing to engage in a discussion within a system geared to separate rather than to bring together, or to foster a belief that one is right and the other is wrong, or to advocate that one is more deserving than the other, it naturally stimulates our survivor instincts rather than the truth of our heart. A silent conscious thought transmitted from our heart-space — *"I honor the place in you in which the entire universe dwells. I honor that place in you, which is of love, of truth, and of peace. When you are in that place in you, and I am in that place in me, we are one"* — will shift the energy in the room and open the hearts of all who are present.

## *The Actual Settlement Conference*

As you enter the room for a real settlement conference, silently offer the Namaste greeting and imagine your intention filling the room and the hearts of everyone present. It is important to maintain alignment with your higher self and your connection with your guides throughout the process. Listen not only with your physical ears to what is being said, but also listen from your soul for quiet messages, thought patterns, and other symbols that may be communicated during the process. Tune into your body, and ask yourself these questions: "Am I aligned? Am I in a state of equilibrium? Is the energy flowing freely through me? Is this resonating with my truth?" Feel into the answers to these questions.

Allow your body to communicate with you. If something does not resonate with your truth, you may feel a pit in your stomach or some other obvious physical manifestation. Your intuition responds to you subtly — pay attention to your first instinct, prior to giving your logical mind a chance to interfere. If you find yourself wanting to defend, argue, or if you feel any fear-based emotion, you are out of your power. Just notice that you have temporarily slipped to the back seat and allowed your ego to take the wheel. In these moments, place your physical hands on the physical table in front of you, and as you do, imagine that you are placing your hands on the surface of the crystal table from your focused meditation and allow its vibration to help you recover your alignment.

Silently restate your intention and feel yourself anchored back into the energy of your pre-settlement exercise. If necessary, ask for a break so that you can breathe, bring yourself back into alignment, and communicate with your higher self and your guides. This is not a time to drop the ball and allow your ego-mind permission to negotiate on your behalf. This is the time to ask for assistance, step back into your power and proceed when you feel connected. If you must imagine touching the crystal table or need physical breaks multiple times to maintain your alignment and connection, that is all right.

The more preparatory work you have done, the more you will be able to maintain your vibration, regardless of the activity in the room. Your intention for a high-vibrational solution requires that you maintain your energy at that same vibration. Once you drop into the ego and lose your power, you will vibrate at a much lower frequency. If this happens, and the energy is not consciously shifted, you will find yourself in a meeting where the energy of fear rather than the energy of love is dominant. Be mindful that there are only love and fear in the universe. Anything not birthed from our highest expression and true essence of love is birthed out of fear.

The negotiation process, by its nature, is dualistic and involves two opposites, no matter how "soft" the approach. Every physical manifestation begins with energy. Thus, to achieve a solution that is outside the lower vibrational field of forced compromise — the battle between right and wrong, fair and unfair — you must strengthen your constitution and allow your guides and the universe the proper platform from which to co-create with you. Do not feel pressured that you alone are charged with controlling the energy of everyone in the room. Rather, you are only responsible for you. If you do your part, you can rest in the knowing that your higher self, your guides, and the Divine Source will do the heavy lifting.

## *Decision Making*

In addition to managing your energy throughout the divorce process, particularly during a settlement conference where important, long-lasting decisions will be made, you must be masterful in the ability to discern your own truth. You are encouraged to ask yourself questions such as, "What do I believe to be true? What is precipitating this decision? Am I making this decision from a place of integrity, from a place that reflects my truth or am I simply regressing into a familiar pattern? Am I fully aligned as I make this decision? Am I holding tightly to my need to be in control, or demanding that I receive every answer to my 'what if' questions, or am I amplifying my faith and belief that if I follow my truth, all will be well, all is well?" It is important to answer these questions as they relate to each decision that will be woven into the tapestry of your divorce settlement.

Just as the scent of a strong perfume will remain long after the wearer leaves the space, when decisions are out of alignment with our truth, the residue lingers like a virus that spreads and feeds on itself. At times, such misaligned decisions can trigger feelings of self-loathing and anger, and anger is an energy that craves expression. As we drift further and further out of alignment, the saboteur within us is awakened.

When a decision is made from a place that does not resonate with our truth, we are foolishly abandoning our knowing and negotiating with fear. Similarly, when we make choices with the sole intention of "making peace" with another or with a situation, but the choices are against our own truth, the intended equilibrium cannot occur. Moreover, if we disregard our soul's nudges in the process, any lesson or issue intended for us to experience will remain in the shadows. It is vital that all decisions are made from a place that can be sanctioned by the soul. If the ego mind is offered the opportunity either to share in, or to override, the decision-making process, there is a risk that one will regress into old illusions.

Knowing that your divorce is a pivotal time in your soul's evolution, the inner work you do and the decisions made during this period, will either help you leap forward on your journey and into the future life you have envisioned, or they will simply reset the stage for you to explore and honor your truth from new experiences and relationships that bring recurrent themes. This discussion does not imply that you should insist that all issues be settled on your terms alone, for that is indeed a proffer of the ego. It simply means there is a fine distinction between a decision made from the ego and one engendered from a place of alignment that speaks to our highest truth.

From here, we are free to create new paradigms, and to invite in new energies, new experiences, new vibrational frequencies that are more representative of who we have become — the current version of ourselves — rather than continuing to occupy the space of our past experiences. We can lay down the worry that old energy is waiting to tap us on the shoulder for another round. When we learn that the "what-ifs" we are so fond of giving our energy to are simply smoke and mirrors, we can blow the smoke to the side and proceed from a place of clarity.

Always remember that your Spirit team is with you during your divorce, just as it has been with you for each experience of your journey thus far. Everything we do in life is for the experience, the learning, the wisdom, the creation, the discovery of who we are, to know our power intimately, and to use it to propel us forward in gratitude and fearlessness. We are never alone. Your Spirit team is so close to you, you can feel them in your heart — with each step and each breath you take, each decision you make, each tear you cry — they are right there with you. Each prayer or request you make for assistance is heard and responded to. Your team is always present, and cheering you on. They dance with joy for you, they send their love to you, they send healing energy and light to you. They send you guidance and gratitude as you proceed on your path. Your team in Spirit knows that your divorce is a critical point in your journey. If it is handled with care, if you allow yourself to engage in the inner work as you proceed through the transition, your Spirit team will work with you, support you, and celebrate your progress. There is no graduate or certification program that will provide you with more pride for your achievements than that of your own inner University of Evolved Understanding.

# 21

# Divorce Ritual and
# Soul-to-Soul Divorce Decree

**J**ust as you engaged in certain rituals when you were married, it is important that you engage in your own sacred divorce ritual, whatever that may mean to you. In the beginning of the divorce process, your ritual may be to allow yourself a brief period to cry, to laugh, to reminisce, to feel angry, to play the victim, to play the hero or heroine, to have a toxic drink of self-pity, to ask another to listen to and validate your story, whatever you feel you need to punctuate this moment of your journey. However, once you have experienced this "no counting calories period," the true ritual begins. It is important to immediately dive into the inner soul work and preparation exercises that are necessary for you to consciously move forward. At the end of the divorce process, it is important to gift yourself a proper closure to the experience.

The concept of a divorce ceremony has gained popularity over recent years. It is seen as a mindful honoring of the rite of passage that divorce presents and provides the closure missing in the legal/civil divorce process. You will be provided with a judicial Decree of Divorce at the completion of your divorce process that terminates the matrimonial bonds of marriage. While this Decree of Divorce represents a limited physical closure to your human legal ties with your spouse, this process does not provide emotional closure, nor does it bring closure to the souls' relationship. The receipt of a certified, earthly-based, legal divorce decree is devoid of both the acknowledgement of, and the direction for, the souls' relationship post-divorce.

There are many options for a divorce ceremony. A public ceremony, which might include family, friends and the children of the marriage, allows divorced parties to publicly announce their divorce and the transition of their family. It can be performed at a location having special significance to them. It is a moment to honor the love and the life the parties enjoyed during their marriage, and marks the end of a cycle and the beginning of a new cycle for each party. When the parties married, the marriage symbolized the coming together of two people into a union of marriage; a divorce ceremony allows for public recognition that each party is leaving the marriage as a whole person. Pronouncing that each party is deserving of dignity and respect and wished well for their individual journeys, a divorce ceremony sanctions each party's continued relationships with friends and family members.

The parties might each write new vows to each other, expressing what they loved about their life together, and their commitment to a transformed relationship as friends and loving co-parents for their children. Friends and family members, including the children of the marriage, might participate in such a ceremony to make statements of encouragement and commitment to honor, respect and support the parties divorce. Some divorce ceremonies might include a symbolic cutting or breaking of an item into two separate pieces with words and actions of the parties and other attendees serving to symbolically connect or weave the two pieces together in honor of the newly formed relationship. It can be very healing for children to witness their parents honoring the loving and sweet memories of the marriage, forgiving and releasing the negative, and making a commitment to love and honor each other under the umbrella of a new relationship. Such ceremonies can be performed with or without a formal officiant.

There are many who are not comfortable with the idea of a public display of their divorce ceremony, and prefer a more private ritual. Private divorce ceremonies have been popular for many years. In these cases, a letter or new vows that may be privately exchanged between the divorced parties could include positive memories about the marriage, what each of them loved about their life together, an expression of gratitude, a statement concerning forgiveness, their commitment for the future relationship, if applicable, and a statement of good wishes for the future of their former spouse. This exchange can either be done together in a private ceremony, or the writing and the exchange of the document will serve as the complete ritual. The parties may even allow their children to read the documents, which may provide needed healing and closure for them as well.

For those who prefer a more personal and private ritual, an intentional stroll through a labyrinth can be very healing. The labyrinth symbolizes that life is a journey of discovering change and transformation. During the walk, allow yourself to have a soul-to-soul communication with your former spouse for the purpose of closure and healing. Breathe in and silently express the goodness and the blessings of the marriage as you walk forward; as you reach the end of the path, consciously release all that needs to be released. A private moment lighting a candle can symbolize the honoring of the past with gratitude and embracing the new journey ahead. Blowing out the candle can symbolize your conscious letting go of all that needs to be released.

Another approach is to memorialize positive memories and the blessings of the marriage in writing on a piece of paper or separate cards and then write down the events which triggered pain, hurt, anger and other negative memories on another piece of paper or separate cards. In a private ritual, or with anyone you desire in attendance to witness this moment with you, you can include flowers, candles, photos, whatever you are guided to include in your personal ritual. The paper or cards reflecting the negative memories of the marriage can be burned or ripped and discarded in running water or any other form of destruction to symbolize your release and intention to alchemize these negative memories and emotions into the love of the Divine Source.

The positive paper or cards can be saved with your formal divorce documents to symbolize the sacred closure of the end of a cycle and your commitment, prayer and hope for your journey ahead. If you have engaged in the inner work suggested in this book, the private or public ritual you choose at the end of the divorce process will be more meaningful, uplifting, and graceful. In fact, you may have already accomplished the healing and closure you need. In this case, your post-divorce ceremony will be designed for the benefit of family, friends, and the children of the marriage, and will provide you with additional confidence and pride regarding how far you have come.

Finally, whether you engage in a divorce ceremony or not, I recommend you compose a Soul-to-Soul Divorce Decree to symbolize the understanding and recognition of the soul-to-soul relationship with your former spouse. The ending of a physical union does not terminate the spiritual connection and the fullness of the legacy between you. To fully heal, we need to step out of our human perspective of the relationship and honor the relationship at a soul level, particularly if there are children involved.

If you have done the inner work, you will be cleared, healed, poised and ready to move forward with your new vision and a fresh perspective. You will put a first foot back on the soil of your soul's path with peace in your heart, a sense of accomplishment and pride, and a curiosity and excitement for what is next to come. While others may flounder for years in the aftermath of the divorce experience, you will take with you only the lessons, blessings, and wisdom, the *jewels* of both the marriage and the divorce process. You will become a beacon of light for those who will come after you — those who may learn and be enlightened by the walk of wisdom you have trod with a brave and open heart.

### *Soul-to-Soul Divorce Decree*

The following sample is just one of many soul-to-soul decrees that could be composed by those who will be co-parenting with their former spouse, post-divorce.

This sample may also be modified to accommodate any continuing relationship, post-divorce. It is important to allow your words to flow from your own inner wisdom, and to be sure you are fully aligned with your higher self before you begin. This decree should be in your own handwriting and stored with your legal decree of divorce. After a period of quiet contemplation and/or meditation, begin by stating your intention for your Soul-to-Soul Divorce Decree. Allow your intention to come about organically. Your higher self and the guides who have been with you throughout this journey will be assisting you. For this sample, we will use the names, "Sarah" and "Michael" to represent the divorced parents, and "Max" and "Zoe" to represent their children. This sample is offered as Sarah's Soul-to-Soul Divorce Decree; however, the process is meant for everyone.

### Sarah's Soul-to-Soul Divorce Decree

"Comes Now Sarah, with the human costume I wear removed. I come from the light of my soul to set forth this decree to the soul of Michael. Although our human contract together as husband and wife has been dissolved, our souls' journey continues — for our own evolution as well as the well-being and evolution of the souls of our children. It is with humility and grace that I state the following:

I, Sarah, hereby decree that I shall make a concerted effort to remain consciously aware that we are each on a soul journey, and we are here to fulfill our individual missions. I will always remember to gift our children, Max and Zoe, with a unified presence, even during those times where it might seem impossible. I shall honor your role as an invaluable parent to our divine children; their well-being shall be the vanguard of each interaction and co-parenting decision made. I will treat you, Michael, with the respect and dignity you deserve as a divine being of light and will silently remind you of my own divinity when such is necessary. From this moment forward, I will remember our souls' connection in the Spirit world and will consciously intend that the space that divides our two individual lives be filled with the light of that divine connection. May this light be a constant reminder that our earthly life together has been transformed, but our "family" will remain strong. I send gratitude and love to all aspects of our souls' past, present, and future interconnected relationship. I intend that the healing that transpired during our physical divorce process will serve to heal and shape all journeys that we have traveled or will travel together. All is right with my soul; may all be right with your soul; and may the souls of our children be eternally blessed from the love and modeling they receive from our evolved relationship."

Signed this _____ day of _____, 20____.

_____
Sarah

## *Affirmation of Release*

The following Affirmation of Release is an example you can use to assist in releasing all that is no longer serving your highest interests. This affirmation, or another of your own creation, should be placed in a prominent space where you will be reminded to acknowledge and repeat it often, until you have an inner knowing that you have truly released what is no longer serving you, and the wings of your soul are unfettered and ready to soar. If you will be co-parenting children and/or maintaining a future relationship with your former spouse, the intention is to amend the soul contract rather than terminate it. You can include a statement recognizing this amended contract within your affirmation, knowing it has been, or is in the process of, being revised by your higher self and the higher self of your former spouse, even if you are unaware of the exact provisions. Trust that your intentions are heard, and that you are both receiving the assistance you need.

*It is my intention to use my divine power and psychic scissors to remove all vows, contracts and agreements which I have made in this lifetime as well as in every other time-line in every dimension, past, present and future, which is not serving the highest good for the evolution of my soul. To all karmic bonds, past, present and future, known and unknown, I acknowledge you and give gratitude for all you have gifted to me and to my soul's evolution. I now forgive you. I release you, and I set you free. You are no longer a part of my energy field. You are alchemized into a blank slate of pure potential from which I will continue my jour-*

ney. I send you off to be transmuted into the purest light of the Divine Source. I affirmatively retain the wisdom I have gained from all experiences, and I forge ahead with curiosity, courage, and the wonderment of my inner child...

**And so it is!**

# 22

# Divorce in the Age of Aquarius

Ihave included this extra chapter for those interested in the
Age of Aquarius, and perhaps how this new era might affect
their lives and their divorce. As this project nears completion,
we are in the year 2020. Although there is no dispute that
we are moving from the Piscean Age and into the Age of
Aquarius, there is little consensus about whether we have
already reached the moment of the shift. There are some
who proffer that the shift took place in the year 2012, a date
consistent with the end of the Mayan calendar. It is believed
that, by ending their calendar in the year 2012, the ancient
Mayan civilization was depicting the end of the Piscean Age
and the birth of a new era as opposed to the doom and gloom,
end-of-the-world prophesy that gained a popular following.
There are others who believe there is enough evidence to
prove we have been on the cusp of the Aquarian Age since
the mid-twentieth-century mark, and perhaps as far back as
the French Revolution. Still others believe we will not fully
enter the Age of Aquarius until approximately the year 2600.
It is my belief that, just as the influence of a zodiac sign makes
itself known several degrees before the date the actual shift

takes place, we are indeed feeling the orb of influence of the Aquarian Age. The December 21, 2020 grand conjunction of Saturn and Jupiter in the sign of Aquarius, occurring for the first time in eight hundred years, could certainly be deemed a divine cosmic push in that direction. The light from this conjunction will certainly serve to usher many individuals across the threshold of their awakening.

We understand that the earth rotates on a tilted axis, and that, due to the gravitational influences of the moon and sun, the earth's axis rotates through a conical precession known as a tremble or wobble every 25,920 years. This movement has been broken down into twelve parts that are linked to the signs of the Zodiac. Accordingly, the influence of each Zodiac sign lasts approximately 2,160 years. We know that the earth's orientation has been influenced by the energy of Pisces for roughly two thousand years, and that the Age of Aquarius is believed to begin when the point of the March equinox moves out of the constellation of Pisces and into the constellation of Aquarius. Because there is a lack of consensus among astronomers and astrologers as to the actual date we entered the Piscean Age, it is difficult to pinpoint the exact commencement date of the Aquarian Age.

Aquarius, the eleventh sign in the Zodiac, can provide us with an orientation of what we can expect as we continue our movement into the Aquarian Age. The number eleven is the first of three master numbers in numerology, and, in part, represents spiritual awakening and an intimate connection to the Divine Source. Aquarius is the sign of the future — it represents freedom and liberation. Those born under the sun sign of Aquarius are free thinkers, socially conscious, inventive, humanitarian, and philanthropic. They are open to new ideas and new ways of doing things. They are the voice of invention, revolution and thought, and are known for their interest in the evolution of humanity.

Accordingly, in the Aquarian Age, we can expect to see more individuals developing an inclusive, global view, as opposed to a parochial concept limited by the boundaries of one's own habitat. Looking for and creating solutions with a higher purpose and broadened perspective, more individuals will be joining together with inspired action. Aquarians understand the concept of collaboration. It is only through a collaborative effort — without judgment, embracing compassionate action — that meaningful change can be accomplished. In the age of Aquarius, we will not be content with a structure that fails to serve everyone. For those who follow and believe in astrological mysticism, the Aquarian Age will bring in the higher understanding and harmony that has been lost in previous eras and will awaken the higher mind.

We can see signs of the Aquarian Age in how we are beginning to treat divorce. More and more people are awakening and looking for a better way to divorce — a harmonious uncoupling. The use of mediation and the collaborative process, as opposed to traditional litigation, are growing in popularity. These processes were developed and used by those who have evolved beyond the battlefield approach, and each provides compassionate methods that honor the dignity of the divorcing couple and respect their desire for a gentler approach. Moreover, these processes assist in the healing process by focusing on the future interests of the parties rather than highlighting and breathing new life into the old negative patterns of the marriage.

On a broader scale, when we look back to the mid-twentieth century, we can see that we have been moving in the direction of personal transformation and taking small steps in the areas of civil rights, racial equality, woman's rights, LBGTQI rights, animal rights, and the dissemination of information. The 1960s Hippie counterculture was a movement against the control of the establishment and a search for truth, freedom, and a world without pain and suffering. Regardless of whether one appreciates the bohemian lifestyle choices of the Hippies on their quest for utopia, the yearning for a new way of living was clearly present.

As more women found success climbing the corporate ladder, it became possible for women to become the primary family breadwinner. Simultaneously, parenting roles also began to shift as more men began to assume the primary childcare responsibilities. We have seen a movement towards respect and acknowledgment for individual choices in the evolution of the laws allowing for same-sex domestic partnerships and marriages. Information, networking, and the disclosure of secrets in all areas will be the hallmark of the Aquarian Age. As more individuals awaken to who they really are and allow their divine inner guidance to lead them, the fear-based grip of hierarchical structures of organized religions, large corporations, banking systems, and other forms of dominion over the population will further weaken.

A new "world family" was born in the 1990s with the advent of public access to the World Wide Web (Internet), which had its military roots in the 1960s. Individuals from all over the world were able to connect to each other instantly. The search for information and connection became a fast-food, instant gratification proposition. No longer were we guessing or assuming what others across the oceans were thinking or experiencing. No longer exclusively dependent upon the media, we went right to the source. Online, we were able to witness the happy cries of the human spirit's need for connection as well as the desperate cries for understanding and compassion. There has been a surge of hope that, as a collective, we would acknowledge how similar we really are, in terms of our basic needs and desires. Despite the censoring actions of patriarchal governments and corporations that remain in control of Internet access, the creativity and tenacity of the Aquarian Age is clearly shining through. We have witnessed millions of individuals liberate themselves from traditional forms of employment to become entrepreneurs who are creating their own livelihoods. This would not have been possible for most without this Aquarian Age invention.

In the year 2020, we saw a powerful resurgence of the impetus for change through the "Me Too" and "Black Lives Matter" movements. These movements, along with a push to continue working for restorative justice, shined a spotlight of awareness that penetrated the collective consciousness. Through the power of social media, another Aquarian Age tool, events are no longer isolated to a local venue; each event is becoming a global event. The voices of the masses are becoming louder as the desire to live in a world where compassion, empathy, inclusion, and acceptance, rather than judgment and exclusion, is heightened. One by one, individuals are breaking through imaginary glass ceilings. More are coming out of their shells and speaking their truth. Rather than facing criticism, they are receiving acceptance for their individual expressions of the Divine Source. The box of limitations and cultural shaping of one's reality is beginning to vanish as we begin to understand the ancestral wounds and expectations that have followed us for generations. With the awakening of one individual at a time, our personal and collective slumber is indeed coming to an end.

The more the light is shined on the shadow of our collective consciousness, the more we can expect the grip of those in power to tighten. This shift will take more than the simple flipping of a switch. Change comes gradually. To experience a flourishing equilibrium across the collective, we must all exercise patience and be willing to make our own contributions in whatever way we are nudged to do so. It will take generations to fully experience the highlight of the Aquarian Age; however, we are here now to shepherd in this energy and to begin shaping the world into the paradigm we wish to experience. As Mahatma Gandhi observed: *"We but mirror the world. All the tendencies in the outer world are to be found in the world of our body. As a man changes his own nature, so does the attitude of the world change towards him. This is the divine mystery supreme. A wonderful thing it is, and the source of our happiness. We need not wait to see what others do."*

When the predominant dependency on outside sources is dismantled, there will naturally be a period of uncertainty. When the chokehold of fear and control are released, like the earth's axis, humanity too will experience a period of wobble. As with our personal relationships, there are times when languishing in the familiar, however uncomfortable, appears safer than what is unknown to us. Fear may be present in those who lose the foundation they have depended upon, and to which they have become accustomed. We have witnessed the growing pains of transformational change, with a rise in suicides, addictions, terrorism, and even new forms of inequality.

It was anticipated that the year 2020 would be a year of 20-20 vision. What we saw and experienced was a world that was compelled to take a pause. It was as if humanity was forced into a dark night of the soul. An invisible virus, known as Covid-19, had the power to literally stop the world. The virus not only exposed the survival instinct in every human being, but also shined a light on the old energies, the old structures, and the prisons in which we have been residing, both internally and externally. We were forced to step back from the energy of "doing" and compelled to simply be.

In this period of involuntary introspectiveness, we began to evaluate our individual lives in terms of what is important to us. Are we living consciously, or are we creatures on the hamster wheel of what society has conditioned us to believe is living? What does life mean to us? What does successful living look like? Are we joyous in our living, or are we battered into a life of submission and order? Despite the number of jewels and wealth we may have accumulated, most of us have walked the earth with a void in our heart. Our outer jewels may sparkle, but our inner treasure is left unseen and unattended to. More and more we are reaching our hands out to each other with an acknowledgment that we are all in this together, that we are all united and connected by the umbilical cord of our Divine Source. We have never been so dependent upon the survival of others to secure our own survival. No matter what we have been programmed to believe, we are all a part of a larger tapestry, we all are deserving of love, compassion, fairness, abundance, and most importantly, a peaceful, joyous life experience.

Nothing has ignited a sense of unity such as what was created by the Covid-19 virus. There was no one on the planet who was immune to, or was able to avoid, the higher purpose of, the infiltration of this boundaryless virus. For a moment, everyone on the planet was united with the recognition that we are interconnected as one family. Color, nationality, political preferences, religious associations, belief systems, distribution of wealth and caste systems, royalty, and all other forms of disparity became far less relevant.

For a time, we were able to view our planet from a unified lens. From our still isolation, as our hearts bled, we saw how connected we really are. Despite the instinct of the population to hoard food and other goods for their own survival, there has never been a time when the love and compassion of humanity was so greatly highlighted. Parades of gratitude filled the streets in celebration for those who were in selfless service to others — those who risked their lives and those who lost their lives in striving to help others survive. The spirit of the Aquarian Age was alive in the faces and hearts of those in service. These individuals mirrored on a grand scale what unconditional love and compassion, selfless service and concern, collaboration and appreciation really mean, and what we are — at our core.

Opportunities to go in the direction of our highest good can, at times, be isolating, fearful, and downright painful as they force us into a humble surrender. However, it is up to us to put one foot in front of the other, to ask for guidance and to bravely move ahead. Humanity has experienced the most humbling surrender of our time. The 2020 Covid-19 pandemic will be known as one of the great triggers of the greater awakening. Even those of us who have been spiritual seekers for many years will be forever changed and expanded. We will look back at the many illusions we continue to carry in our energy field, things we thought we had integrated and released, only to find that were still holding on to their roots as a form of security.

Those living at the time of the 2020 pandemic and the generations that will follow, will be the souls who will help define the new world. We all played a role in designing and shaping the age we are shedding; it is up to us to be the enlightened evolutionaries for the future. We chose to be here, to participate in, and to experience change in whatever form it might manifest. We must honor our decision to be here at this time and to fulfill our mission of planting and nourishing the seeds for the harvest of the new world — and to be the lighthouse that illuminates the path for others who are just awakening. From our individual rise of consciousness to the collective rise in consciousness, we are ready to take the next step of our evolutionary journey.

It is through our intention and the awareness of who we are that we will create. We are called to hold the vision of a healthy world. We must also each reconnect with the soul of Mother Earth and give her the reverence she deserves. The Gaia theory, proffered in 1970 by James Lovelock and Lynn Margulis, that the earth is an intelligent, living being, who self-regulates the elements to sustain life upon her, is now accepted as fact. Ancient civilizations considered the earth as a sacred mother providing life and nourishment to her children. Every culture has recognized her existence in some fashion, and some have given her distinct names — "Gaia" by the Greeks and "Pachamama" by the Incas. Prior to becoming reduced to a myth, the Mother Spirit of the earth was worshipped and appreciated for the love she embodied, the wisdom she shared, the resources she provided, and the magical way in which she created an equilibrium from which every living creature could survive and thrive.

The consciousness of the earth is a part of the awakening phenomenon. She is not separate from us; she, too, is woven into the collective consciousness and connected to the Divine Source. The earth's frequency has an influence upon our health and well-being; and, conversely, our collective frequency has an influence upon her. The earth is a conscious being and can be strengthened or weakened by our collective vibration and behavioral choices. Thus, as we evolve, we allow the earth to evolve. Humanity has moved away from the native practice of appreciating earth's cycles and needs and treating her as a partner, as a fellow traveler. When we begin to acknowledge her as a partner, we will again remember how she freely provides her abundance to sustain us and protect us during our human sojourns.

We must individually and collectively continue to use the wisdom we have gained as a catalyst for our own individual growth and the evolutionary growth of the collective. As we begin to learn that the currency of love is our most valued commodity, we will all be charged with reaching out and taking the hand of another — for on this mission, there will be no one left behind. The Divine Source operates from the frequency of love, and therefore, the frequency of love is our most natural state. We are asked to progress to a mentality where love, rather than fear, guides all action. As the softer, healing attributes of the feminine begin to blend with its masculine counterpart, an equilibrium will emerge. This blending of the feminine and masculine energies in terms of the collective consciousness will be vital to the creation of a balanced society.

As evolved and awakened people are drawn to public office, they will foster a new form of democracy, a spiritual democracy, in which the soul of every human is honored, respected, and understood to be part of the collective brotherhood of light. They will have mastered their ability to use their intuition as their compass, and will make decisions from a heart-mind connection for the citizens they represent. Together, we shall stand in appreciation of our differences, with an understanding that we are all expressions of, are connected to, and have a direct contact with, one Divine Source. There will be no need for dogma, propaganda, and other forms of suppression to feed a need for power. With knowledge that the only real or meaningful "power" lives within each one of us, the old paradigms will lose their appeal.

As humans, we have become accustomed to living our lives on the wheel of karma. The karmic system or paradigm has dictated our purpose, our emotions, our relationships, and our experiences. Lifetime after lifetime has been guided by karmic influences. Many of us have reached a level of consciousness and understanding that it is within our power to remove ourselves from the cycle of karma because it serves no purpose for our evolutionary growth. We can terminate the karmic cycle by simply intending it. As more and more individuals jump off the wheel of karma in their search for truth, freedom, and ascension, it is inevitable that we will experience a period of confusion and chaos. What will life look like without the karmic push? If a child is told that he or she can do anything at all, in many cases, that child will simply stare into space in a state of confusion.

As the familiar structures of our civilization are changed (and, in some cases, eliminated) over time, there will be periods of uncertainty and adjustment. There is, in fact, no model or prototype for the next phase of human evolution. We are creating the template by our intentions, our thoughts, and our actions. While many are awake and ready for change, many are resistant to change, whether consciously or subconsciously. This reality may in fact keep the wheel of karma spinning for some time.

As our civilization evolves, the way we handle disputes must also evolve. For those families caught in the web of the traditional legal system, much could be improved upon. For the family in transition, the traditional courtroom-and-litigation model has such high (and avoidable) potential for harm to that family and to the human spirit. Marriages and divorces will continue to be a part of the human experience. A decision to end a marriage should receive the same dignity and respect provided to those who decide to begin a marriage. As more divorcing couples learn that they have a choice in how they handle their divorce — and do so successfully — the faster the word will spread. As more individuals are willing to use their divorce as a catalyst for their own souls' evolution, others will be inspired to do the same. Positive outcomes always inspire followers. Once the vibration of the divorce process is elevated, the denser energy that is related to the stigma and shame of divorce will also experience a shift. Organizational and cultural paradigms, as well as the court system, will accordingly evolve; in the meantime, it is my hope that as many people as possible are spared the intrinsic sting of the process.

The "Great Awakening" is not a mystery to which only a few are privy. We are all part of this awakening process. There have been many definitions and theories proffered about this period in our human evolution. Simply, the Great Awakening is the discovery of truth — our truth — that we are divine beings of light. We are all divine spirits living a human experience. We must also awaken to the true power within us. As the dormant strands of our DNA come back online, we will be reunited with our full potential.

We are equipped with the ability to heal ourselves, and with the ability to connect with the intelligence of the quantum field. We are equipped with the ability to create anything into physical form, and with the gift of telepathy, pre-cognition, and teleporting. We are equipped with the ability to extend our life far beyond its current life span. These gifts or abilities were demonstrated by Yeshua, or Jesus, as well as others who came with similar messages. As more truths are revealed about humanity's true origin and our intimate connection to a much larger galactic family, our perspective on life and how we fit into the larger picture will also evolve. Shifting dimensions is simply a shift in consciousness, a shift in our awareness, and the discovery of the dormant gifts and abilities inherently present within each of us. As our gifts and abilities are further revealed to us, we will begin to remember the depth and breadth of who we really are.

We must remember we are free — free to express our light in any manner we choose. Once we release the self-imposed limitations of our human experience, we discover that we co-create our own experiences. Together, we have created the current human condition — with all its ups and downs, joys and sorrows, equities and inequities. We have the power and free will to move the pendulum of experience to a more benevolent state that is more consistent with our own divine nature. Awakening does not mean that we must sacrifice our most sacred beliefs; rather, we are meant to master the ability to blend that which we cherish with our own truth — to question everything from the perception of our own divinity. A return to our own sovereignty broadens our perspective and naturally fosters a reverence for the sovereignty of all others. Judgment, greed, deception, the need to control others, and all other fear-based behaviors lose their luster as the light of the energy of love and unity becomes the dominant influence.

Change will indeed take time. But we can accelerate the process by remaining conscious of our thoughts, feelings, words, and actions. No matter what is happening around us, we must view it all from the eyes of the observer and not get tangled up in the minute details of every single event. No matter how big or small they appear, we must treat all experiences the same. Observe them as if we are observing someone else's life. When we are engrossed in the scene of a movie as an observer, we find ourselves offering advice to the characters as though they can hear us. We never consider how silly we appear in that moment of innocence. When we can observe ourselves and the events of our life from that perspective, we place our higher wisdom into a direct channel from which to speak to us. Without the fear, doubt and worry clouding our connection, we can stay aligned with the wisdom present in each encounter. We must hold our knowing that the Divine Source is benevolent. For when we stand in our truth, we are always provided for.

As you proceed through your divorce process, stay mindful of the bigger picture, for yourself and for those who travel behind you. Be mindful that our individual choices absolutely affect the whole. We must proudly and bravely hold the torch of love high in all our endeavors. It is in this way that we bless our own soul's journey, make our contribution to the journey of the human collective, and dearly bless the path of those who will walk behind us. We must not forget that we are also preparing the field for ourselves should we choose to return. We are creating new archetypes and paradigms, rather than living within the constraints of those we have already experienced. This is an internal shift — as many have observed before us, we are "who" we have been waiting for. May we walk proudly, confidently, and peacefully with that knowing. With all endings come new beginnings. The pen of creation is now in our hands; let us write well.

I am so grateful that you have allowed me to share in your journey. May you go in peace knowing that all is well with your soul. I leave you with the words of Dr. Antony Theodore:

*"Once a student asked her Guru, 'What is the difference between one who has wisdom and knowledge and someone who is enlightened?' The Guru responded, 'It is very easy; the one who has wisdom and knowledge is the one who carries the candle in the darkness and lights the way. The one who is enlightened has become the torch itself.'"*

*Note from the Author:*

If you found the information in this book useful to your journey, please consider helping to spread the word by leaving a review at your place of purchase. Reviews are significant feedback, not only important to authors, but also to buyers on their search for knowledge, support, and guidance.

I would love to hear how this book touched and helped you. Please feel free to reach out to me at Pamela@BridgestoSpirit.com.

# Acknowledgments

I would first like to thank my dearest friend, Charles. We have shared many high moments on our journey, as well as some of the lowest moments either of us has known. I will forever be grateful for your love, support, and hours of encouragement and assistance you generously provided to see me through this project. Thank you for listening to my ideas, talking through my frustrations, reading, and sometimes rereading, the chapters, and understanding and believing in the higher purpose of this project.

I would also like to thank my beautiful and talented daughter, Sherri. From the moment you were born, you have blessed my life with meaning, and continue to be my greatest accomplishment. From the precious little girl who held the hand of her teen mother, to the amazing woman you are today, I could not be prouder of you. I know it was not always easy walking (and sometimes stumbling) on this journey together, but thank you for choosing me, we did it! Jordan, Skyler, and Aramis, each one of you hold the trinity of love in my heart. I could never have imagined the extent of blessings that grandchildren bring. May your cups always overflow with the abundance this life has to offer.

To my former clients who have inspired me to continue to push through the traditional constraints and expectations of divorce, your loving spirits have paved a road for others.

Thank you for allowing me to guide and support you through your family's transition. Your courage and willingness to allow intuitive guidance and inner reflection to shape your divorce experience will continue to bestow many blessings upon you as well as upon other fellow travelers who will follow.

Thank you, Paula, for years of friendship, encouragement, guidance, and support. My life has been truly blessed having you, my soul sister, on the journey.

Thank you, Chala, for a lifetime of divine guidance and loving support.

# Bibliography

Amaral, Geraldine; Brady Cunningham, Nancy. *Tarot Celebrations, Honoring the Inner Voice*. York Beach, ME: Samuel Weisser, Inc. 1997.

Amberstone, Ruth Ann and Wald. *The Secret Language of Tarot*. San Francisco, CA: Red/Wheel/Weiser, LLC, 2008.

Domino, Connie. *The Law of Forgiveness: Tap into the Positive Power of Forgiveness and Attract Good Things in Your Life*. New York, NY: Penguin Group, 2009.

Kubler-Ross, Elisabeth; Kessler, David. *On Grief & Grieving, Finding the Meaning of Grief Through the Five Stages of Grief*. New York, NY: Scribner, 2014.

Louis, Anthony. *Tarot Plain and Simple*. Woodbury, MN: Llewellyn Publications, A division of Llewellyn Worldwide, Ltd., 1996, 2012.

Oken, Alan. *Soul Centered Astrology, A Key to Your Expanding Self*. Lake Worth, FL: IBIS PRESS, an Imprint of Nicolas-Hays, Inc. 2008.

Myss, Caroline, PhD. *Anatomy of the Spirit*. New York, NY: Three Rivers Press, 1996.

Pollack, Rachel. *Seventy-Eight Degrees of Wisdom, A Book of Tarot*. San Francisco, CA: Red Wheel/Weiser, LLC:, 2007.

Shah, Nadiya. *Astrology Realized*. Synchronicity Publications, 2013.

Shumsky, Susan. *Ascension, Connecting with Immortal Masters and Beings of Light*. Franklin Lakes, NJ, The Career Press Inc., 2010.

Stone, Barbara. *Invisible Roots: How Healing Past Trauma Can Liberate Your Present*. Santa Rosa, CA: Energy Psychology Press, 2008.

Tanner, Wilma. *Mystical, Magical You*. Columbus, OH: Wild Comet Publishing, LLC., 2004.

Weiss, Brian, *Messages from Masters*. New York, NY: Grand Central Publishing, Hachette Book Group, 2000.

### Internet Reference Sites

Britannica.com
Crystallinks.com/precession

# About the Author

Pamela M. Pacetti is a divorce attorney and mediator. She graduated *cum laude* from The Catholic University, Columbus School of Law in 1998. Known for her signature holistic approach to family law, her passion is to combine her legal knowledge, intuitive abilities, experience and training to help her clients reach uniquely tailored marital agreements, find healing, and achieve a more enlightened perspective on their experience.

An early advocate of the non-adversarial, collaborative divorce process in the Washington, D.C. area, Pamela served as President of the Virginia Collaborative Professionals and, for eleven years, as a board member of The Collaborative Professionals of Northern Virginia. She strongly believes that families in the transition of divorce deserve a process that honors the family and brings dignity and respect to the dissolution of a marriage.

In addition to her legal practice, Pamela is an Intuitive Life, Soul, and Divorce Coach, a Teacher, a Spiritual Medium, a master in Transpersonal Hypnotherapy, and a Quantum Healing Hypnosis Technique practitioner.

Pamela has a beautiful daughter and three delightful grandchildren. A lover of animals and all music, she also enjoys taking daily walks by the ocean. She divides her time between California and the Washington, D.C., metropolitan area.

Made in the USA
Middletown, DE
10 November 2022